A-LEVEL
STUDENT GUIDE

AQA

Sociology

Crime and deviance with theory and methods

Dave O'Leary

HODDER
EDUCATION
AN HACHETTE UK COMPANY

Acknowledgement: The author would like to thank the sociology students at Kingsthorpe College for their support.

This guide has been written specifically to support students preparing for the AQA A-level Sociology examinations. The content has been neither approved nor endorsed by AQA and remains the sole responsibility of the author.

Every effort has been made to trace all copyright holders, but if any have been inadvertently overlooked, the Publishers will be pleased to make the necessary arrangements at the first opportunity.

Although every effort has been made to ensure that website addresses are correct at time of going to press, Hodder Education cannot be held responsible for the content of any website mentioned in this book. It is sometimes possible to find a relocated web page by typing in the address of the home page for a website in the URL window of your browser.

Hachette UK's policy is to use papers that are natural, renewable and recyclable products and made from wood grown in well-managed forests and other controlled sources. The logging and manufacturing processes are expected to conform to the environmental regulations of the country of origin.

Orders: please contact Bookpoint Ltd, 130 Park Drive, Milton Park, Abingdon, Oxon OX14 4SE. Telephone: (44) 01235 827827. Fax: (44) 01235 400401. Email: education@bookpoint.co.uk. Lines are open from 9 a.m. to 5 p.m., Monday to Saturday, with a 24-hour message answering service. You can also order through our website: www.hoddereducation.co.uk.

ISBN 978-1-5104-7204-4

First printed 2020

First published in 2020 by
Hodder Education,
An Hachette UK Company
Carmelite House
50 Victoria Embankment
London EC4Y 0DZ

www.hoddereducation.co.uk

Impression number 10 9 8 7 6 5 4 3 2 1

Year 2024 2023 2022 2021 2020

Cover photo: Dmytro/stock.adobe.com

Typeset by Integra Software Services Pvt. Ltd, Pondicherry, India

Printed in Italy

A catalogue record for this title is available from the British Library.

MIX
Paper from
responsible sources
FSC
www.fsc.org
FSC™ C104740

Contents

Getting the most from this book 4

About this book 5

Content Guidance

Crime and deviance

Sociological theories of crime and deviance. 6

The social construction of crime statistics 14

Ethnicity and crime 16

Gender and crime 18

Globalisation and crime. 21

Green crime 22

Human rights and state crimes 23

The media and crime. 24

Crime control, punishment and victims. 26

Theory and methods

Consensus, conflict, structural and social action theories 31

Modernity and postmodernism. 38

The relationship between sociological theory and methods. 40

Sociology as a science 42

Objectivity and values in sociology 44

Sociology and social policy. 45

Questions & Answers

How to use this section 47

Test paper 1. 55

Test paper 2. 68

Test paper 3. 81

Knowledge check answers 92

Index 93

■ Getting the most from this book

Exam tips

Advice on key points in the text to help you learn and recall content, avoid pitfalls, and polish your exam technique in order to boost your grade.

Knowledge check

Rapid-fire questions throughout the Content Guidance section to check your understanding.

Knowledge check answers

1 Turn to the back of the book for the Knowledge check answers.

Summaries

■ Each core topic is rounded off by a bullet-list summary for quick-check reference of what you need to know.

Exam-style questions

Commentary on the questions

Tips on what you need to do to gain full marks.

Sample student answers

Practise the questions, then look at the student answers that follow.

Commentary on sample student answers

Read the comments showing how many marks each answer would be awarded in the exam and exactly where marks are gained or lost.

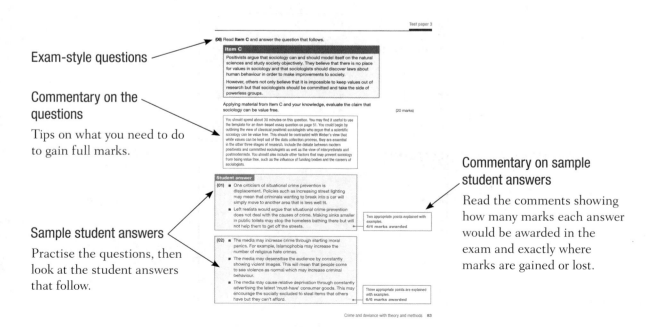

■About this book

This guide is for students following the AQA A-level Sociology course. It deals with the topic of crime and deviance with theory and methods.

There are two main sections to this guide:

■ **Content Guidance** — this provides details of the topics of crime and deviance and sociological theory. There is also a section examining the link between theory and sociological methods. Topic areas on crime and theory examine key ideas and arguments, stating the main points of evaluation, and include the key concepts and key thinkers. The defined words are key words for this specification.

■ **Questions & Answers** — this shows you the kind of questions you can expect in the A-level Paper 3 examination. The questions are followed by sample A*-grade responses.

How to use this guide

When you study crime and deviance topics and theory and methods in class, read the corresponding information from the Content Guidance sections to become familiar with the topic. You should use these sections to complete your own revision notes, for example on each theory and topic within crime and deviance. You should then complete one of the test papers. It is advisable to focus on questions on one topic area, theory or whatever at a time. After you have completed your own answers you should compare them with the sample student answers provided. These and the comments that follow them can be used to amend your revision notes.

The A-level specification is shown in detail on the AQA website: www.aqa.org.uk/7192. Follow the links to Sociology A-level (7192).

Content Guidance

This section outlines the major issues and themes of **Crime and deviance** and **Theory and methods**.

The content of **Crime and deviance** falls into the following areas:
- crime, deviance, social order and social control
- the social distribution of crime and deviance by ethnicity, gender and social class, including recent patterns and trends in crime
- globalisation and crime in contemporary society; the media and crime; green crime; human rights and state crimes
- crime control, surveillance, prevention and punishment, victims, and the role of the criminal justice system and other agencies

The content of **Theory and methods** falls into the following areas:
- consensus, conflict, structural and social action theories
- the concepts of modernity and postmodernity in relation to sociological theory
- the nature of science and the extent to which sociology can be regarded as scientific
- the relationship between theory and methods
- debates about subjectivity, objectivity and value freedom
- the relationship between sociology and social policy

Note that sociological methods, which you will have studied in Year 1, are covered in Student Guide 1, Education with theory and methods.

Crime and deviance
■ Sociological theories of crime and deviance

Functionalism, strain and subcultural theories
- Durkheim (1897) believed that crime was inevitable and would be an increasing problem in modern society as rapid social change and diversity could potentially result in **anomie**. However, he felt that a certain level of crime was a normal part of a healthy society and would lead to various positive functions such as allowing positive social change to occur and acting as a **safety valve** to prevent more serious crime. The criminal justice system and punishment also have the function of reminding people of the boundaries of acceptable behaviour and promoting social solidarity through reaffirming shared values.
- However, Durkheim's theory has been criticised for focusing on social control and conformity rather than explaining why some groups commit more crime than others. Merton (1938) developed a functionalist explanation of crime and deviance and acknowledged that crime could be **dysfunctional** for society. He argued that deviance occurred as a result of the strain between socially accepted goals such

Anomie A feeling of normlessness. Crime and deviance are likely to occur when people are unsure about or are less committed to shared values and rules.

as achieving material success (the American dream) and socially approved ways of achieving these goals such as hard work in school and the workplace.

■ Merton argued that in the USA the main cultural goal was the American dream but that, despite notions of meritocracy, some sections of society lacked the **legitimate opportunity structures** to achieve this goal. This would create anomie for individuals who were excluded from institutional means and would result in crime and deviance (see Table 1).

Table 1 The strain to anomie: Merton's goals-and-means scheme

Response	Goals	Means	Example	Likely social group
Conformity	Yes	Yes	University-educated professional	Middle class
Innovation	Yes	No	Organised crime gang member or petty thief. Commits **utilitarian crime**	Working class (due to inadequate socialisation)
Ritualism	No	Yes	Routine office worker who follows the rules but has no interest in promotion or a career	Lower middle class (may have been over-socialised to conform)
Retreatism	No	No	Dropouts of society	Addicts, 'tramps' etc.
Rebellion	Different goals	Different means	Those wanting to create a new 'social order'	Political radicals and revolutionaries

> **Utilitarian crime** Crime committed for financial gain.

■ **Subcultural** theories of A. Cohen and of Cloward and Ohlin — these developed Merton's notion of **strain** and agree that the lack of **opportunity structures** can be used to explain working-class crime and deviance.

■ A. Cohen argues that working-class boys would value success goals initially but that failure in school due to a lack of legitimate opportunity structures would lead to **status frustration**. As a result of this frustration the boys collectively inverted and replaced middle-class values of educational success with alternative goals and ways of achieving status, such as truanting.

■ Cloward and Ohlin identify three working-class subcultures that result from varying degrees of access to **illegitimate opportunity structures**:

  — **Criminal** Have access to illegitimate opportunity structures and utilitarian crime as they are socialised into a 'life of crime' by members of organised criminal gangs.

  — **Conflict** Have little access to illegitimate opportunity structures due to a lack of organised crime gangs in their area but can achieve status through gang violence.

  — **Retreatists** Have no access to either legitimate or illegitimate opportunity structures. They may have failed in the other two types of subculture and 'retreat' into a world of drugs.

> **Status frustration** When people are dissatisfied with their position in society.
>
> **Illegitimate opportunity structures** Illegal means of achieving success, such as being in a gang and committing crimes such as theft.

Exam tip

Be prepared to link basic functionalist concepts and arguments to their explanation of crime and deviance. As a structural, consensus theory, functionalism argues that crime occurs when social solidarity is threatened by a lack of effective social control mechanisms and when institutions such as the family are failing to socialise people into a shared culture.

■ Miller argues that when working-class men are deviant it is because of their distinctive culture. He argues that lower-working-class culture is characterised by **focal concerns**, which act as a release from the boredom of people's lives and mean that they will inevitably be involved in criminal and deviant activities. For example, the focal concern of 'toughness' will lead to crime such as fighting while 'excitement' will lead to crimes such as joyriding.

Focal concerns The main things that are valued in a culture.

Table 2 Comparison of Merton and subcultural theory

Agree with Merton	Disagree with Merton
Merton and the subcultural strain theories of Cohen and of Cloward and Ohlin argue that working-class people initially share mainstream values of success	Miller's version of subcultural theory states that lower-class culture is separate from mainstream values. It does not share the middle-class goal of the 'American dream'
Merton and subcultural strain theories argue that crime is higher among the working class as they have less access to legitimate opportunity structures such as good education	Cohen and also Cloward and Ohlin argue that working-class people adopt a collective, not individual, response to strain by joining a subculture
Working-class crime is often caused by the need for financial gain. Merton's innovator is similar to Cloward and Ohlin's criminal subculture member, who may commit utilitarian crimes such as burglary	Crime can also be non-utilitarian. Cohen's subculture gained status from truanting and vandalising school property. Cloward and Ohlin's conflict subcultures earned status through winning 'turf wars'
Deviants might 'drop out' of society such as Merton's retreatism response and Cloward and Ohlin's retreatist subculture, whose cultural values may both focus around drug use	Cloward and Ohlin's retreatist subculture members are 'double failures' as they lack access to illegitimate opportunity structures (criminal and conflict subcultures) as well as legitimate ones

Exam tip

To develop analysis, compare Merton's strain theory and subcultural theories with the left realists Lea and Young's version of subculture (see Table 3 on page 13). While they have different views on the causes, both believe that members of subcultures may be unable to achieve society's cultural goals due to blocked opportunity structures.

Interactionist Matza (1971) argues that rather than there being a distinctive subculture, groups in society use a set of deviant '**subterranean values**' that exist below mainstream values. People normally keep these values under control but they occasionally emerge in situations such as after drinking too much at the office party or the end of Year 13 holiday in Ibiza. Matza argues that when this occurs we use **techniques of neutralisation** (sets of excuses) to justify our deviant actions, such as the 'denial of responsibility': 'That wasn't me, I was drunk'.

Evaluation

■ **Merton** Are there just five types of adaptation and common goals in society? The American dream may not be applicable to the UK today.
■ **A. Cohen** Are working-class deviants aware that they are 'inverting' middle-class values? Delinquent behaviour such as truanting may be done just 'for a laugh'.
■ **Cloward and Ohlin** There may be more than three types of subculture and an individual may be involved in more than one, such as a small-time drug dealer who is also a user.
■ **Miller** There is little evidence to suggest that focal concerns are restricted to working-class males. Does a completely separate, homogeneous working-class subculture exist? However, **New Right** sociologists such as Murray (1990) would support Miller's ideas, arguing that there is now a distinct **underclass** whose values encourage deviant and criminal behaviour.

- **Interactionists** such as Matza argue that separate subcultures do not exist and that we all '**drift**' between conformity and deviant '**subterranean values**'.
- **Marxists** argue that strain and subcultural theories ignore corporate crime. Marxist subcultural theorists such as Brake (1980) argue that working-class subcultures, such as punk and skinhead youth subcultures, develop as a resistance to capitalism rather than through strain (see page 7).
- **Feminists** argue that strain and subcultural theories are 'malestream' and ignore female crime and deviancy, such as the increase in 'girl gangs'.
- **Postmodernists** such as Maffesoli (1996) argue that rather than there being rigid subcultures resulting from causes such as strain, young people belong to 'neo-tribes' that are fluid and diverse. Rather than being based on deviant working-class values, neo-tribes result from different lifestyles that are influenced by a range of factors that are often media-led.

> **Knowledge check 1**
>
> Outline two criticisms of subcultural theories of crime.

Interactionism: labelling theory

Interactionists disagree with the functionalist view of crime and deviance in a number of ways:

- Rather than deviance producing social control, interactionists argue that agents of social control are the cause of crime and deviance.
- Rather than using an absolute definition of deviance, interactionists adopt a relative definition and argue that there is no fixed view of what constitutes deviant behaviour. As Matza argues, people 'drift' in and out of deviance.
- Rather than seeing official statistics as reliable and as generally accurate in reflecting patterns of crime, interactionists regard them as being socially constructed and lacking validity. **Phenomenologist** Cicourel argues that due to police using typifications, crime statistics say more about the way the police operate than actual levels of crime.

> **Typifications** Shared concepts used to make sense of the world such as stereotypes that working-class or black people are more criminal than other groups.

Interactionists focus on **labelling theory** and how agents of social control — such as the police, the judiciary and the media — have the power to define less powerful groups as deviant. **Becker** (1967) argues that social groups create deviance by making rules and then labelling those who do not conform to these social controls as 'outsiders'. He argues that '**moral entrepreneurs**' (such as politicians) have power over individuals and are able to redefine behaviour and laws into what they feel is acceptable.

Lemert (1951) differentiates between **primary deviance**, which constitutes deviant acts that have not been labelled, and **secondary deviance**, which is the **societal reaction** caused by acts being publicly labelled. For labelling theorists, societal reaction to being labelled as deviant has many different consequences:

- The individual can be **stigmatised** and excluded from 'normal society', as **Goffman** demonstrated when people are labelled as mentally ill.
- The label can become an individual's '**master status**' — the main way that others see them (e.g. being viewed as a 'junkie' rather than as a father or boss). This is likely to have a negative impact on an individual's self-concept, and a **self-fulfilling prophecy** will occur as they will begin to see their identity in terms of the label.

- **Becker** argues that further societal reaction, such as discrimination in the workplace, may lead to the labelled person following a '**deviant career**', resulting in them joining a subculture with others who have been similarly labelled.
- **Young's** (1971) study of hippy drug users illustrates how aspects of secondary deviancy, such as police persecution and labelling, led to a self-fulfilling prophecy where drug-taking and other subcultural deviant behaviour increased. This process, where labelling and an increased attempt to control behaviour actually create more deviance, is called the **deviancy amplification spiral**.
- **S. Cohen's** (1972) study of mods and rockers (see Table 5 on page 25) is another example of how labelling, in this case by the media, can lead to deviance amplification via a **moral panic**.
- **Braithwaite** (1989) distinguishes between **disintegrative shaming**, where the criminal is negatively labelled and excluded from society, and **reintegrative shaming**, which labels the act as bad but not the person themselves. Braithwaite argues that reintegrative shaming avoids the negative effects of societal reaction and can lead to lower levels of crime, as offenders will be made aware of the impact of their behaviour and will be accepted back into society without being stigmatised.

Evaluation

- + Interactionism illustrates how deviance is a relative concept and how deviance, crime and crime statistics can be socially constructed.
- + It draws attention to the importance of labelling and its consequences.
- + It demonstrates the impact of agents of social control at a micro level and how they may create more deviance.
- – Labelling theory is too deterministic as individuals can reject labels and not follow the deviant career. However, Becker does acknowledge that individuals have the power to resist labels.
- – Labelling theory only focuses on trivial forms of deviance and is not useful in explaining more serious crimes, such as murder.
- – **Akers** (1967) criticises labelling theory for blaming societal reaction for an individual's deviant behaviour. He felt the act itself is more important than societal reaction and that individuals are aware that they are breaking the law.
- – Interactionism fails to explain why people commit deviant acts in the first place.
- – **Left realists** argue that labelling theory is too sympathetic to the criminal and ignores the victims of crime.
- – **Marxists** argue that it ignores the wider, macro origins of labelling and that labelling reflects the power of the ruling class in a capitalist society.

Knowledge check 2

Outline two strengths of interactionist theories of crime.

Marxism

Rather than social control benefiting everyone, as functionalists suggest, Marxists argue that it benefits the ruling class and works against working-class people's interests by preventing them from rebelling against the injustices of capitalism. Marxists agree with interactionist criticisms of the functionalist view of crime and deviance that official statistics on crime are invalid due to the law being selectively enforced by powerful groups. However, traditional Marxists argue that this occurs at a macro rather than micro level. They argue that the structure of capitalist society can be seen to explain the causes of crime in three ways:

1 Capitalism is **criminogenic**. By its very exploitative nature, capitalism results in class inequality and poverty. **Gordon** (1976) suggests that higher levels of working-class crime are a response to this inequality. He argues that the emphasis on greed, profits, competition and materialism means that crime is a rational response by all social classes to capitalism. This is demonstrated in **white-collar crimes**, such as tax evasion and fiddling expenses, and **corporate crime**, such as health and safety violations, share-price fixing and environmental offences caused by pollution. Advertising is seen as encouraging crimes such as theft as a way to acquire the latest 'must-have' goods. Marxists further argue that increasing alienation (see page 33) of the working class can cause non-utilitarian crime such as vandalism and violent behaviour.

2 **Selective law making and enforcement**. Marxists argue that the law reflects ruling-class interest rather than the will of the people as functionalists suggest. **Snider** (1997) argues that laws that threaten the profits of big business, such as fair trade laws and health and safety legislation, are unlikely to be passed or enforced beyond a minimum level. **Chambliss** (1970) argues that laws to protect private property are used by the ruling class to maintain the capitalist economy and keep the working class away from its spoils.

3 **Ideological** functions of crime and deviance. **Althusser** (1969) argues that the law is an **ideological state apparatus** which serves the interests of capitalists by maintaining and legitimating class inequality. Selective law enforcement, such as targeting social security 'scroungers', benefits the rich and powerful — tax fraudsters are rarely taken to court as their crimes are less likely to be treated as criminal offences. **Reiman** (2001) suggests that white-collar and corporate crimes are under-policed and under-punished. **Pearce** (1976) argues that the real purpose of laws seemingly passed in the interest of the working class, such as health and safety laws, is to serve capitalism by helping to ensure safe and loyal workers. The occasional prosecution will give the impression that the law is applied fairly and shows the 'caring side' of capitalism.

Marxists argue that crime statistics will reflect **selective law enforcement** and this, coupled with biased media coverage, will give the impression that crime is a working-class phenomenon. This will result in working-class people blaming working-class criminals for the problems they experience, such as low pay, which capitalism is causing. Conversely, **white-collar crime** and **corporate crime** are not seen as a serious problem by the public despite their being more costly to society. There are a number of reasons for this, such as the invisibility of the offences, the lack of a clear victim or knowledge of the offender. Corporate crime in particular is less likely to be prosecuted for a number of reasons — it is more complex; responsibility for it is often diffused and protected by powerful interests such as the state; it is dealt with internally to protect the company's reputation.

Exam tip

Compare this view of selective law enforcement with labelling theory, which fails to locate it within a wider social context — i.e. how bias in the legal system benefits capitalism.

Exam tip

Be prepared to link points to general Marxist theory. The belief that the law acts in the interests of workers is an example of the false consciousness that Marx argued existed among the working class.

The New Criminology, by **Taylor, Walton and Young** (1973), agreed with traditional Marxists on issues such as criminogenic capitalism and selective law enforcement, but argued that a **fully social analysis** is required. This **neo-Marxist** approach combined the traditional Marxist views on inequality with the micro approach of labelling theory and its emphasis on societal reaction and individual meanings.

The New Criminology is often referred to as **critical criminology** as it argues that the sociology of crime and deviance must be critical of the established capitalist order. It also takes on a more **voluntaristic** approach, arguing that individuals have free will and are able to commit crime for political reasons in response to the injustices of the capitalist system. The New Criminology provides a framework for research based on seven micro and macro factors which were adopted in order to produce a fully social theory. This approach was used by neo-Marxist Hall in his study on black muggers (see the Ethnicity and crime section).

Marxist subcultural theory, developed by the Centre for Contemporary Cultural Studies, argued that working-class youth subcultures developed their styles of clothes, music and language as a form of resistance to social inequality.

- **P. Cohen** (1972) described how 1970s skinheads reacted to the decline of working-class communities through symbols, exaggerating the clothes of the traditional manual worker, such as Dr Martens boots, and asserted their working-class masculinity through football violence.
- **Brake** (1980) argued that such resistance is '**magical**' — an illusion that only appears to solve their problems. He argued that each generation of working-class youth subcultures have resisted their exploited situation though different sorts of music, clothes and so on.
- **Hebdige** (1979) outlined how punks '**resisted through rituals**' by deliberately shocking the establishment through their use of deviant symbols, such as Mohican haircuts, swastikas and bondage on clothing. However, he argued that the deviant styles that subcultures used would soon be commercialised by capitalism and available in high street retailers — such as commercial versions of punks' DIY ripped jeans with safety pins quickly becoming available in Topshop.

Evaluation

- + Marxist theory of crime demonstrates how the law reflects differences in power between social groups.
- + It highlights the impact of selective law enforcement and how corporate and white-collar crime is under-policed.
- + It has drawn attention to how inequality can lead to criminal behaviour.
- – Marxism is too deterministic and does not explain why not all working-class people who experience poverty commit crime.
- – **The New Criminology** accuses Marxism of being **economically deterministic**, arguing that not all crime is caused by economic factors.
- – The assumption that the end of capitalism will lead to the end of crime is rejected. Capitalism does not appear to be criminogenic in countries such as Japan or Singapore, which have a very low crime rate.
- – Traditional Marxist theory has been accused of ignoring the relationship between ethnicity and crime and deviance.

> **Exam tip**
>
> The ideological nature of the law and its selective enforcement can be seen in Hall's book *Policing the Crisis*. This examined the moral panic about mugging in the 1970s, when the media scapegoated black muggers for the problems in capitalism at the time. Hall argued that this had the effect of dividing white against black working-class people, who were blamed for the problems in society, rather than capitalism.

- ■ – **Left realists** argue that, by focusing on the crimes of the powerful, Marxists neglect the fact that working-class people are the main victims of working-class crime.
- ■ – **Right realists** agree and also argue that Marxism is too critical of the role of the police and the courts, which are a necessary part of social control.
- ■ – **Functionalists** would argue that the law is applied equally and that there are numerous examples of the criminal justice system (CJS) acting against the interests of the ruling class, such as MPs' expenses.
- ■ – **Feminists** argue that different types of Marxist theory ignore the patriarchal nature of the law and social control.
- ■ – The New Criminology group only provided a framework and did not conduct any research themselves. The 'fully social analysis' they advocated incorporates seven aspects of crime that were very complex.
- ■ – The New Criminology has been criticised for its emphasis on the political nature of crimes, which is not useful for explaining crimes such as domestic violence and child abuse.
- ■ – Marxist subcultural theory has been accused of underestimating how far youth subcultures are influenced by the consumerism and popular culture of the USA, such as 'gangsta rap' and 'Nike identities'.

Realist approaches to the causes of crime and deviance

Table 3 Similarities and differences between right and left realists

| Similarities | Differences on the causes of crime | |
Ideas	Left realists	Right realists
Crime is a real, growing problem that is damaging communities, particularly in urban areas	**Relative deprivation** Due to the media and consumerism, we are more aware of how deprived we are in relation to others. This may lead to crime as people feel resentment when they think others 'unfairly' have more than them, e.g. stealing the latest iPhone	**Biological differences** Wilson and Herrnstein (1985) claim some people are naturally more aggressive, more extrovert and of low intelligence and so commit more crime due to biologically determined factors
Individualism and the pursuit of self-interest lead to the breakdown of family structure and the community and can lead to crime	**Marginalisation** Groups such as unemployed youth and minority ethnic groups may feel powerless as they have no one to represent them (leading to social exclusion). They may turn to crime such as vandalism or violence out of resentment or frustration	**Socialisation** Some families, particularly lone-parent ones, fail to teach correct values such as self-control, often due to the lack of a male role model. Murray (1990) felt that there was a growing underclass who did not share the values of society and so were more likely to commit crime
Realists agree that labelling and different Marxist theories are too sympathetic towards the working-class criminal	**Subculture** As a consequence of relative deprivation and marginalisation, some working-class and black people may seek a collective response and form deviant subcultures. Due to their blocked opportunities, some may turn to street crime	**Rational choice** Clarke (1980) argued that individuals rationally choose to commit crime because the costs are outweighed by the benefits. Felson (1998) argued that if a motivated offender was in the presence of a '**capable guardian**' they would act rationally and not offend

Knowledge check 3

Outline two criticisms made by left realists of Marxist theories of crime.

Exam tip

Relate right realism to the New Right views of Murray on the importance of the nuclear family and on it being undermined by the welfare state, creating a dependency culture. It is argued that social policies on reducing dependency, such as cutting benefits, can also reduce crime by encouraging individuals to be more self-reliant. Working people will be financially independent and less likely to be involved in street crime.

Exam tip

While right realists generally argue that poor values cannot be changed, Wilson and Herrnstein (1985) argued that individuals with a biological predisposition to commit crime can be 'trained away' from it with the right socialisation. However, the underlying causes of crime are very difficult to change.

Exam tip

For a question on the views of realist theorists on the causes of crime, be prepared to refer to their different crime prevention strategies (see the section on realist approaches to crime prevention).

Evaluation

- + Left realists have drawn attention towards the reality and fear of crime that exist for some deprived groups.
- + Both realist theories have been influential in social policies aimed at tackling crime (see the section on realist approaches to crime prevention).
- − **Hughes** (1991) argues that left realists fail to explain why some people who are relatively deprived commit crime and others do not.
- − By focusing on property crime and inner-city crime, left realists fail to provide evidence to support a representative theory of crime.
- − Left realists' use of subcultural theory and the assumption that crime occurs when there is no value consensus has been criticised. **Marxists** would argue that left realism has strayed too far away from Marxist views in adopting functionalist concepts to explain crime.
- − **Lilly et al.** (2002) reject the biological argument of right realists. They found that only 3% of differences in offending could be explained by differences in intelligence levels.
- − While rational choice may be useful to explain some utilitarian crime, it cannot explain violent crime and crimes committed under the influence of alcohol or drugs.
- − There is a contradiction between criminals making rational choices and having low intelligence and being poorly socialised.
- − **Marxists** and **left realists** argue that right realists ignore wider structural causes of crime such as poverty and social exclusion.
- − **Marxists** argue that both realist theories neglect corporate crime, which is more damaging to society.

Knowledge check 4

Outline two areas of agreement between left and right realists.

■ The social construction of crime statistics

- Police crime statistics have been collected since 1857 and are now published quarterly by the government. The statistics are useful in showing patterns and trends in offending. However, there are a number of reasons why official crime statistics (OCS) may not show the real rate of crime:
  1 Crime may not be reported to the police for a number of reasons, such as fear of reprisals, distrust or lack of faith in the police, the trivial nature of the crime, and embarrassment.
  2 The police do not record all crimes due to reasons such as a lack of evidence, offences seen as too trivial, and the negative impact on their clear-up rates and chances of promotion.

- Another way of estimating patterns of offending is **victim** (or victimisation) **surveys**, in which individuals are asked for details about crimes committed against them, typically in the last year. The **British Crimes Survey (BCS)**, now called the **Crime Survey of England and Wales (CSEW)**, has been conducted by the government since 1981 and includes a large sample (now around 50,000 people).

- Both OCS and the BCS have revealed that crime increased rapidly between the mid-1980s and 1993 but has decreased since then. Figures from the CSEW in 2015 showed a 7% decrease in crime compared to the previous year, and the lowest estimate since the BCS began in 1981. Between 2015 and 2019 there has been no significant change in crime rates. The findings of the BCS/CSEW suggest that only a quarter of crimes are reported to the police, illustrating that police-recorded crimes may be only the tip of the iceberg in the case of some crimes.

- The BCS/CSEW and other victim surveys have revealed that the 'fear of crime' is increasing, particularly for those living in socially deprived areas. Despite the evidence to the contrary, two thirds of the respondents to the BCS/CSEW consistently state that they believe crime has increased a little or a lot over the last 15 years.

- Lea and Young used their own victim survey, the Islington Crime Survey (1986), to illustrate their 'realist' approach and to demonstrate that the fear of crime was a genuine fear among working-class people and other marginalised groups living in deprived areas. Unlike other Marxist-influenced approaches to crime, they argue that official statistics do reflect real patterns of crime.

- Despite the BCS/CSEW being more valid than OCS, as it includes crimes not reported to the police and so shows the **'dark figure of crime'**, it has a number of drawbacks:

  1 It does not survey all crimes. For example, it excludes theft committed against businesses, corporate crime and victimless crimes such as prostitution.

  2 It only recently included those under 16 years of age.

  3 People may not be aware that they are a victim of crime, e.g. children or in crimes such as fraud.

  4 Victims' memories of crime may be inaccurate, e.g. due to the trauma experienced.

  5 Despite the survey being anonymous, people may not admit to being victims of crimes such as sexual offences.

- **Self-report studies** ask respondents to reveal crimes they have committed and provide another useful alternative to OCS. For example, they reveal that middle-class males are just as likely to offend as working-class males. However, these studies may lack validity due to respondents believing that their crimes might be reported to the police.

Dark figure of crime
The unknown amount of crime that is never revealed. This applies more to crimes that are less visible, such as white-collar crime, and crimes of a sexual nature such as rape.

Exam tip

For an essay involving theoretical explanations of crime for both class and ethnicity, be prepared to refer to the methodological approach adopted by left realists Lea and Young.

- OCS suggest that crime is largely a working-class phenomenon. The vast majority of the prison population are from socially deprived backgrounds and most people who appear in court are from working-class backgrounds. As has been outlined in the previous section, different sociological theories have different explanations regarding why members of the working class appear disproportionally in OCS. While those who adopt a positivist approach, such as functionalists, accept the validity of OCS in showing a realistic picture of crime, theories based on an interpretivist approach argue that OCS are **socially constructed** and are based on the institutional biases of the criminal justice system. Marxists would agree that the law is selectively enforced and would argue that offences associated with the middle class, such as white-collar crimes, are largely ignored, whereas working-class offences, such as street crime, are targeted by the police.

> **Knowledge check 5**
>
> Outline two strengths of victim surveys.

Summary

After studying these sections, you should be aware of sociological explanations of crime, deviance, social order and social control. You should be familiar with the following:

- functionalism, strain and subcultural explanations
- Marxist and neo-Marxist explanations
- labelling theory and the social construction of crime
- right and left realist approaches to the causes of crime and deviance
- sociological explanations of patterns of crime in relation to social class, e.g. selective law enforcement and white-collar crime
- different methods of measuring crime: official crime statistics, and victimisation and self-report surveys

■ Ethnicity and crime

- Black people, and to a lesser extent Asian people, are over-represented in OCS at all stages of the criminal justice system (CJS). In 2019, people from BAME (black, Asian and minority ethnic) backgrounds made up 25% of the prison population but only constituted 14% of the general population. Black people accounted for 13.7% of the prison population but only made up 2.7% of the general population. Conflict theories, such as interactionism and Marxism, argue that such statistics reflect levels of discrimination towards minority ethnic groups (MEGs) rather than real rates of offending and have made several criticisms of the CJS.
- **Phillips and Browning** (2007) argue that MEG communities are likely to feel 'over-policed and under-protected'. This is reflected in statistics from 2018 showing that black people are eight times as likely (and Asian people three times as likely) as white people to be **stopped and searched** by the police. Phillips and Browning suggest that as a result of this deliberate targeting by the police, some black people act out the label of potential criminal and commit street crime.

- **Holdaway** (1983) observed a **canteen culture** in the police that was racist and influenced officers' decisions to stop and search black people. Following the inquest into the death of the young black teenager Stephen Lawrence, the **Macpherson Report** (1999) concluded that there was **institutional racism** in the Metropolitan Police.

- However, the **demographic explanation** argues that statistics may just reflect the fact that MEGs are over-represented in population groups most likely to be stopped and searched, such as young people in inner-city areas. Waddington et al. (2004) found this to be the factor that shaped stop and search policies of the police rather than any racial discrimination.

- There is also evidence of racism in the **judicial process**. Hood (1992) found that black males were more likely to receive custodial sentences than white males for the same offences. While Asian people and black people are less likely to be found guilty than white people, this may be because police stereotyping leads to cases being brought to court against MEGs with weaker evidence.

- Victim surveys also tend to suggest higher rates of offending by black people. They also show a high level of intra-ethnic crime (i.e. crime that takes place within ethnic groups). Self-report studies, however, do not support the view that black people are more likely to offend than white people, and also show that Asian people are less likely to offend.

Table 4 applies theories of crime and deviance to the issue of ethnicity and includes the two main explanations for ethnic differences in crime statistics, neo-Marxist and left realist. For more detail and evaluation of these theories, refer back to the section on sociological theories of crime and deviance.

Canteen culture A term used by Holdaway to describe the occupational culture within the police force that was characterised by racist (and sexist) attitudes.

Exam tip

Be prepared to link moral panics to a discussion on the social construction of OCS in relation to MEGs. In addition to Hall's moral panic, refer also to how the post-9/11 moral panic of Islamophobia may have contributed to the police targeting Asian people. For example, Asian people are three times more likely to be stopped and searched under the 2000 Terrorism Act than any other group.

Table 4 Sociological explanations of ethnicity and crime

Theory	Explanation	Key concepts/studies
Functionalist	Lack of goals or institutional means. MEGs innovate due to the racism they experience	Merton — MEGs experience **anomie**
Right realist (New Right)	Due to poor **socialisation** and in some cases being in a lone-parent family, some MEGs may be more likely to be part of an underclass and live a life of crime	Murray (1990) Underclass Dependency culture
Interactionist	MEGs are more likely to be negatively **labelled** by agents of social control, and therefore appear disproportionately in crime statistics	Phillips and Bowling (2007) Labelling and self-fulfilling prophecy
Marxist	MEGs are more likely to be working class and commit crime targeted by agents of social control	**Selective law enforcement**
Neo-Marxist	1 *Policing the Crisis* — The police released statistics suggesting that black Britons were more likely to be involved in street crime. Black youth was a **scapegoat** used to divert attention away from the problems of capitalism. This led to more aggressive policing, e.g. stop and search policy 2 Gilroy — 'The myth of black criminality'. Police target young black Britons. Their crime is **politically motivated** and is a reaction to racism	1 Hall (1978) Moral panic (black muggers). Black youth portrayed as a folk devil via **media labelling** 2 Gilroy (1982) **Police labelling** Institutional racism
Left realist	OCS reflect real differences in MEG offending. Structural opportunities for MEGs are blocked by racism, which leads to **social exclusion**. As a result MEGs are more likely to feel poor and turn to crime, often with other like-minded people, e.g. in street gangs	Lea and Young (1993) — MEG crime is caused by: ■ relative deprivation ■ marginalisation ■ criminal subculture

Evaluation

- Left realists reject interactionist and neo-Marxist views that OCS are socially constructed and instead argue that they reflect real fears, e.g. about mugging. They argue that while police racism exists, it cannot on its own explain ethnic patterns of crime, such as why conviction rates for Asian people are lower than those for black people.
- Hall has been criticised for assuming that white working-class people were 'panicking' and blaming crime on black people and for not explaining how the moral panic was created.
- Gilroy's view of black crime as being political has been criticised for failing to acknowledge that most black crime is committed against other black people and therefore cannot be politically motivated.
- Left realists have been criticised for underestimating the impact of police racism. For example, there has been an increase in the Muslim prison population from 7.7% in 2002 to 16% in 2019, which conflict theorists would argue is linked to Muslims being viewed as the new 'enemy within' by the authorities since 9/11.

Knowledge check 6

Outline two ways in which it has been argued that the CJS is racist.

■ Gender and crime

Female crime

- According to the Prison Reform Trust, women made up less than 5% of the prison population in 2019. In 2018, males accounted for 85% of all arrests made. There are significant gender differences in offending. Males are much more likely to be convicted of violent or sexual offences whereas 82% of females entering prison in 2018 had convictions for non-violent offences. Theft and handling offences were the two highest offences for which women received custodial sentences.
- One explanation as to why women appear less in the OCS is the **chivalry thesis** developed by **Pollock** (1950), which argues that the CJS is more lenient towards women. This is due to males being socialised into being protective towards females.
- Evidence from self-report studies supports the view that women are treated more leniently. **Campbell** (1981) and **Graham and Bowling** (1993) both discovered that females committed a lot more crime than the OCS suggested. Campbell also found that women were more likely than males to be cautioned for committing the same offence.
- However, evidence from **Box's** (1981) self-report study suggests that women who commit serious offences are not treated more leniently than males. Farrington and Morris (1983) found that this was also the case in magistrates' courts.
- In terms of sexual offences, evidence suggests that the CJS is biased *against* women. **Casborn** (1985) and **Heidensohn** (1996) found that courts are more severe on female juveniles when it comes to crimes related to sexual promiscuity. **Walklate** (2001) argued that in rape cases it is often the female victim rather than the male offender who is on trial.

Knowledge check 7

Outline two criticisms of the chivalry thesis.

- Whether chivalry in the CJS exists is open to debate, but it is clear that women have a lower offending rate than males. A number of explanations have been put forward for this:

  1 **Functionalist sex role theory** Parsons (1955) argues that differences in crime and deviance are due to **differential socialisation** in the family, such as girls being brought up to fulfil the expressive role and boys being encouraged to be tough and take risks. While early feminist explanations such as those of **Smart** (1977) accept the significance of differential socialisation, they argue that it reflects patriarchy and needs to be changed. Feminists are also critical of functionalists for basing their ideas on biological assumptions about females being more naturally responsible for caring for others.

  2 **Patriarchal control** Heidensohn (1985) argues that women have fewer opportunities to commit crime because they are socially controlled by patriarchy. This happens in three ways:
     - **In the home** Due to the traditional roles of housewife and mother, women have less opportunity for crime. Daughters are also more closely controlled in the family, for instance being given less freedom to go out at night.
     - **In public** Women are less likely to go into public places where deviance occurs, particularly at night due to a fear of violence such as sexual attacks. Women's behaviour is also controlled through the fear of acquiring a bad reputation, such as being a 'slag' or 'bitch'.
     - **In the workplace** Women's lack of opportunities in the workplace, illustrated by the gender pay gap and the glass ceiling, mean that women will have fewer opportunities for crime, particularly white-collar crime. Heidensohn quotes research which found that as many as 60% of women have suffered some form of sexual harassment at work, showing this to be another form of patriarchal control experienced by many women.

  3 **Class and gender 'deals'** Drawing on **Hirschi's** (1969) control theory (see the section on realist approaches to crime prevention), **Carlen** (1988) argues that working-class women commit crime only when they lack the controls that prevent most females from doing so. The two main controls are the **class deal** (financial security) and the **gender deal** (emotional attachment to family life). In a study of 39 women who had been convicted of crime, 32 had always been in poverty (lacking the class deal) and most had either been in care or had experienced some form of sexual violence (lacking the gender deal). Carlen concluded that for these women, crime was a rational response to the lack of class and/or gender deals and was the only route to a decent living. Both Heidensohn and Carlen combine feminist and control theories to explain why females commit less crime. However, as Heidensohn acknowledges, control theory can be criticised for portraying women as passive victims. As well as being dated, Carlen's study is small-scale so may not be representative.

Exam tip

Be prepared to apply other functionalist-based arguments to a discussion of gender and crime. Subcultural theorists such as Cohen and Miller argue that the culture and values of working-class boys lead to crime and deviance. Also, New Right thinker Murray argues that the lack of a male role model in single-parent families can encourage males to take up criminal behaviour.

Exam tip

Be prepared to evaluate more 'dated' explanations with contemporary evidence. As a result of this type of control, McRobbie (1978) argued that girls developed a bedroom culture which restricted their opportunities for crime. Since then there has been an increase in girl gangs, and in addition, the advent of online gaming has arguably led to a bedroom culture for boys, who may be socialising with friends at home or online rather than 'on the street'.

4 **Liberation theory** According to **Adler** (1975), increasing rates of female crime can be explained by women's liberation. As society becomes less patriarchal, women will have greater confidence and opportunities to commit the same crimes as men. Denscombe (2001) suggests that young females are engaging in more risk-taking behaviour and are adopting more traditionally male attitudes such as 'looking hard'.

5 **The feminisation of poverty** Rather than liberation, some feminists point to the increased marginalisation of women since the 1980s as they have become more likely than men to experience poverty due to low pay and benefit reductions. Heidensohn (2002) argues that most female criminals are working class and commit crimes such as shoplifting and prostitution out of economic necessity rather than liberation.

Exam tip

While sociologists tend to reject biological factors, they cannot be ignored and could be discussed briefly in an essay on gender and crime. For example, premenstrual tension has been accepted as a form of defence in courts since the 1980s.

Masculinity and crime

- **Messerschmidt** (1993) argues that crime and deviance are one way that men can accomplish masculinity. The dominant form of masculinity that boys are socialised into is **hegemonic masculinity**, which stresses differences from women and is defined by goals such as: being a breadwinner; having power over others, particularly females; treating females as sexual objects; toughness and risk-taking behaviour. Some men may not want to achieve these goals (e.g. gay men) or may be unable to achieve them and may turn to crime to accomplish different (or subordinated) masculinities. For example, white working-class males who may underachieve may develop anti-school cultures based on toughness or non-conformity to achieve a **subordinated masculinity** in school, whereas black working-class boys may turn to violent street gangs outside of school.

- Messerschmidt notes that middle-class men may also be motivated by a masculine value system but will turn to white-collar or corporate crime to accomplish hegemonic masculinity.

- Messerschmidt has been criticised for not explaining why only a minority of men turn to crime to accomplish their hegemonic masculinity goals. It is also argued that masculinity may be just one way that crime is expressed, e.g. toughness, rather than being a cause of crime.

- In the late (or post) modern era, **deindustrialisation** has meant that some working-class men can no longer achieve their masculinity through traditional forms of employment. **Winlow**'s (2001) study of bouncers in Sunderland illustrates how the 'night-time economy' has provided them with opportunities to demonstrate their masculinity through violence as well as additional 'perks' to their paid work in the form of money through illegal activities such as drug dealing.

Deindustrialisation
The process whereby the traditional manufacturing sector in countries like the UK has declined, due to the growth of the global economy. This has cut the number of manual jobs, leading to unemployment, poverty and crime.

Summary

After studying these sections, you should be aware of the social distribution of crime and deviance by ethnicity, gender and social class, including recent patterns and trends in crime. You should be familiar with the following:

- patterns of crime in relation to gender and ethnicity
- sociological explanations of patterns of crime in relation to ethnicity, e.g. racism and the criminal justice system
- sociological explanations of patterns of crime in relation to females, e.g. the chivalry thesis, sex role theory and feminism
- sociological explanations of patterns of crime in relation to males, e.g. masculinity and crime

Globalisation and crime

- Globalisation, the increasing interconnectedness of societies, has been spread by a number of factors such as the growth of global media, global markets, mass migration and tourism. **Held et al.** (1999) suggest that globalisation has led to the spread of transnational organised crime, creating new opportunities for existing crime but also creating new ways of committing crime. For example, greater communication and travel have enabled the drugs industry to transcend national boundaries. Other examples include human and arms trafficking, cybercrime, green crime and international terrorism.

- In 1988 **Castells** suggested that the global criminal economy was worth over £1 trillion per year. The illegal drugs trade illustrates how global criminal networks have developed to meet the demands of the West. The supply of drugs is met by farmers in countries such as Colombia, who will make more money growing illegal crops to meet this demand than by growing conventional crops. As a result, cocaine production outsells all of Colombia's other exports combined.

- **Hobbs** (1998) argues that crime is no longer just local but '**glocal**', as it involves networks of people across the globe. Rather than being based on old mafia-style fixed hierarchies, criminal networks are increasingly more fluid. As well as drugs, other examples of glocal trade are trafficking women and children for prostitution and slavery, and smuggling legal and stolen goods to sell on foreign markets.

- **Glenny** (2008) traces the spread of modern transnational crime to the break-up of the Soviet Union and Eastern bloc and the simultaneous deregulation of global markets. In Russia this created opportunities for a new capitalist class (often ex-Communist officials) to make vast sums of money selling the country's natural resources, such as gas, on global markets. To protect their wealth these 'oligarchs' turned to new '**McMafias**', comprised of ex-Communist secret service employees, police and former criminals. Again, these criminal networks were not organised like the traditional Mafia, and groups such as the Chechens would even 'franchise' their business to other parts of the globe.

- From a Marxist perspective, **Taylor** (1997) looks at the impact of transnational corporations (TNCs) on global crime. Globalisation has allowed TNCs to more easily switch production to developing countries. This not only exploits workers in low-wage countries but creates unemployment and poverty in countries from which

Knowledge check 8

Outline two ways in which the 'McMafias' differ from the Mafia.

production has shifted, leading to an increase in domestic crime. Deregulation and the fact that global crime is difficult to police have made it easier for elite groups and TNCs to commit crimes such as tax evasion.

- **Beck** (1992) argues that the new insecurities of the late-modern era have led to a **global risk consciousness**, in relation to threats such as migration or global terrorism. The public demand to deal with such risks, often fuelled by sensationalist media coverage, has led to Western governments increasing methods of social control, for example through tighter border controls and the use of surveillance technology (see the Liquid surveillance section).

Green crime

- Green crimes are crimes against the environment. These crimes can have a negative impact on both humanity and the environment.
- Due to **globalisation**, green crime is on the increase as a result of the planet being a single ecosystem. Environmental disasters, such as the nuclear accident in Chernobyl and the BP oil spillage in the Gulf of Mexico, are not restricted to nation-state boundaries.
- **Conflict theorists** such as Marxists would argue that green crime is largely committed by powerful groups such as BP and other TNCs that work hand in hand with powerful elites, e.g. politicians in government.
- **Late-modern** theorist **Beck** argues that we are living in a '**global-risk society**' that has been brought about by efforts to meet the increased demands for consumer goods. The resultant increase in production has led to 'manufactured risks', such as the increase in greenhouse gas emissions which contribute to global warming.
- **Green criminology** transgresses (oversteps) the boundaries of **traditional criminology**, which only studies patterns and causes of law-breaking. Radical criminologist **White** (2008) suggests that current laws are inadequate and that green crime should be defined as any crime that causes harm even if it is not illegal. He argues that green crimes such as deforestation of the rainforests are not being adequately dealt with by internal law, due to the influence of TNCs such as McDonald's.
- White also argues that green criminology takes an **ecocentric** view, which sees environmental harm as being interconnected with the future of human well-being. This contrasts with the **anthropocentric** view favoured by TNCs that humans have a right to exploit the resources of the planet, including animals, for their own benefit.
- **South** (2008) suggests that there are two types of green crime:
  1. **Primary** green crimes are the direct result of the destruction and degradation of the Earth's resources, e.g. air pollution, deforestation, abusing animal rights and water pollution.
  2. **Secondary** green crimes involve the flouting of existing laws and regulations, e.g. dumping toxic waste and breaching health and safety rules, such as in the cases of Bhopal and Chernobyl.

Exam tip

Be prepared to relate the impact of globalisation on domestic crime to Lea and Young's left realist explanation of the causes of crime. Increased job insecurity resulting from globalisation and deindustrialisation will lead to a lack of the legitimate opportunity structures required to achieve the material goals of society. This, alongside advertising of global consumer products that the socially excluded cannot afford, is likely to increase feelings of relative deprivation, which may lead to crime.

Evaluation of green crime

- + Green crime draws attention to the increase in manufactured global risks and global environmental concerns.
- + It identifies the need to address the impact of environmental damage to both humans and the other species on the planet.
- – Green crime's emphasis on harm means that it is based on subjective opinions. There are no clear boundaries in terms of defining or studying green crime.

Knowledge check 9

What is the difference between traditional and green criminology?

■Human rights and state crimes

- State crimes are illegal activities that break national or international laws and which are carried out by or on behalf of governments. **McLaughlin** (2001) outlines four types of state crime:
  1 Political crimes, e.g. corruption and censorship of the media, carried out by politicians and civil servants
  2 Crimes by the police, armed services and secret services, e.g. deaths in police custody, torture and ethnic cleansing
  3 Economic crime, e.g. official violations of health and safety laws
  4 Social and cultural crimes, e.g. institutional racism
- **Schwendinger** (1970) argues that crime should be viewed as a violation of people's basic human rights, not just the breaking of laws, and that definitions of state crime should include human rights crimes. He suggests that states are guilty of committing crimes if they deny people equal opportunities by practising imperialism, racism, sexism, homophobia and economic exploitation.
- However, critics argue that Schwendinger's definition of human rights is too broad as he suggests that any violation of human rights should be defined as illegal. **S. Cohen** (1996; 2001) is critical of Schwendinger's view that state crime should include violations of human rights. He argues that there is no clear agreement that practices such as economic exploitation are criminal. There is also limited agreement on what counts as human rights. Cohen also argues that, due to the power of governments and their ability to conceal and legitimate their crimes, the extent of state control is difficult to measure and, as a result, such crime is more 'invisible' than conventional crime.
- Cohen applies Sykes and Matza's **techniques of neutralisation** (see the Functionalism, strain and subcultural theories section) to examine how the state justifies its crimes against human rights. For example, the Nazi concentration camp guards would use 'denial of responsibility' by claiming that they were simply obeying orders. Government secret services may 'appeal to higher loyalties' by imprisoning people without trial in the name of national security.
- Critical criminologists such as Marxists would argue that powerful groups within the state are able to define their activities as legal. For example, as well as having the power to cover up their crimes through issuing legal restrictions on the media, governments are able to define what counts as a war crime. The use of military

Knowledge check 10

Outline two criticisms of Schwendinger's view that definitions of state crime should be extended to include human rights crimes.

Exam tip

Be prepared to link the topic of green crime to a question on state crime. Marxists would argue that state and green crimes often both involve crimes of the powerful. For example, nation-states can use their power to make laws in their own interest about what constitutes environmental harm.

torture and the invasion of countries such as Iraq can be portrayed by UK and US governments as a necessary part of the 'war on terror'.

■ Critics of this view would argue that so-called state crimes are not in fact criminal. They would reject the notion of 'state crime' and would argue that acts such as increased censorship and the curtailing of the human rights of suspected terrorists are necessary if committed in the national interest.

The media and crime

Media representations of crime

■ Interactionists argue that rather than being objective and impartial, the news is socially constructed and is dependent to a large extent on the **news values** of journalists and other media personnel. A key news value that helps to explain why crime and deviance make up such a large and disproportionate amount of news coverage is 'negativity': bad news is good news.

■ However, as **Felson** (1998) states, media reporting of crime is distorted, and he argues that it reinforces a number of fallacies or falsehoods about crime. These include: all age groups are involved in crime; middle-class people are more likely to be victims of crime; the police are more efficient than they seem; and criminals are ingenious rather than opportunistic. Felson argues that the dramatic fallacy exaggerates violent and extraordinary crimes, promoting a fear of crime, particularly among vulnerable groups such as elderly people and women. Such fallacies are reinforced by fictional representations of crime in television programmes, e.g. by the emphasis on violent and sexual crimes in crime dramas.

The media as a possible cause of crime

■ There has been much debate as to whether media content can have a negative effect on the behaviour of the audience, particularly vulnerable groups such as children. The **hypodermic syringe model (HSM)** argues that there is a direct correlation between violence and antisocial behaviour portrayed in film, song lyrics and computer games.

■ **Newson** (1994) argues that long exposure to violence over the course of young people's lives has led to them becoming desensitised to violence, i.e. they have become socialised into accepting violent behaviour as normal. However, **Buckingham** (1993) claims that children are media literate and are able to differentiate between fictional violence in computer games and real-life violence. **Cumberbatch** (2004) reviewed over 3,500 research studies and felt that the evidence on the impact of media violence was inconclusive.

■ In addition to imitation of violence, the media have been seen to influence crime and deviance in a number of other ways, such as glamorising crime and providing information on how to commit crime. **Jewkes** (2003) also draws attention to how new types of media such as the internet have led to new opportunities for crime, particularly cybercrime such as e-mail scams, data theft and illegal pornography. Jewkes also points to how new technology has given governments greater powers of surveillance, such as CCTV cameras and digital fingerprinting (see the Liquid surveillance section).

News values The guidelines used by journalists and other media personnel to determine whether a story is newsworthy, i.e. interesting enough to attract readership or audience.

Exam tip

Be prepared to relate the left realist arguments to a question on the relationship between the media and crime. As well as media representations contributing to a 'fear of crime', Lea and Young point to the role the media play in causing relative deprivation. For example, the advertising of 'must-have' consumer goods further marginalises socially excluded groups, who may then be more likely to turn to crime.

Moral panics (MPs)

Interactionists argue that media labelling can cause crime through what **S. Cohen** (1972) described as a moral panic (MP). Cohen argued that MPs can lead to **deviancy amplification**, as occurred in his study of mods and rockers following the Easter bank holiday of 1964 — see Table 5.

Table 5 The stages of an MP as illustrated by Cohen's study *Folk Devils and Moral Panics*

Stage	Cohen's mods and rockers
1 Media report on an event in an exaggerated way	Newspaper headline: 'Youngsters beat up town'
2 Reporting demonises the group as folk devils using **symbolisation**	Young violent rockers in leather jackets. Mods on customised scooters
3 Moral entrepreneurs react to the media reports	Politicians call for a crackdown on young thugs
4 The media predict further trouble	More violence at the next bank holiday
5 The authorities stamp down hard on the group	Greater police presence and more arrests
6 The group reacts to this response	Gangs become more deviant due to over-policing
7 The self-fulfilling prophecy and the **deviance amplification spiral** are complete	More arrests made and two distinctive youth subcultures formed

There are a number of sociological explanations for the formation of moral panics.

- Cohen argued that MPs occur at a time of 'moral crisis' when society is undergoing major social change. The media portrayed members of the new 'immoral' youth subcultures as **folk devils**, as they were viewed as challenging the traditional authority that they felt 'decent' people should subscribe to.
- **Functionalists** view MPs as a way in which society responds to **anomie** brought about by rapid social change. By focusing people's attention and moral outrage at the behaviour of the folk devil, the media can help uphold social solidarity and ensure that the public demand action to re-establish the status quo.
- **Neo-Marxist Hall** (1978) argues that MPs have ideological functions. He argues that the MP over black muggers divided the white working class against the black working class and, as a result, diverted attention away from the problems that were being faced by capitalism at the time (such as high unemployment).
- **Left realists** reject the view that MPs are simply the result of ruling-class ideology or the result of the biased news values of journalists. They argue that MPs reflect real concerns of marginalised groups, such as those living in inner-city areas.
- An alternative view is that journalists create MPs to sell more newspapers when there is a lack of news stories available.
- The strength of MPs from an interactionist perspective is that they have identified the role of the media in the social construction of crime and deviance.
- **McRobbie and Thornton** (1995) are critical of MPs and argue that they are outdated. With the advent of new technology, such as 24-hour rolling news, they are becoming harder to sustain. It is argued that in the late-modern era, MPs have less impact as the audience is now more active and able to challenge and reject media presentations of the news.

Exam tip

Be prepared to make the connection between moral panics and interactionist theory. You should understand and be able to apply concepts used in the description of MPs, such as labelling, self-fulfilling prophecy, moral entrepreneurs and deviance amplification. These could be applied to a question on crime and deviance and also to a 20-mark question on social action theory.

Knowledge check 11

Outline two criticisms of moral panics.

Summary

After studying these sections, you should be aware of globalisation and crime in contemporary society; green crime; human rights and state crimes; and the media and crime. You should be familiar with the following:

- how globalisation has created new opportunities for and ways of committing crime, e.g. transnational organised crime, global criminal organisations and crimes of the powerful
- different types of green crime and green criminology
- human rights and sociological explanations of state crime
- media representations of crime, and the media as a cause of crime and moral panics

■ Crime control, punishment and victims

Realist approaches to crime prevention

Both right and left realists see crime as a real and increasing problem. While both feel that governments need to adopt practical strategies to reduce crime, they have very different solutions.

Table 6 Realist solutions to crime

Similarities	Differences	
	Left realists	Right realists
Need to get tough on crime	Need to get tough on the causes of crime	Crime cannot be solved, just controlled
The fear of crime is a rational response. Official statistics are reliable and show real patterns of crime and victimisation	**Social and community crime prevention (SCCP)** Policies need to tackle the root causes of crime, such as poverty and social exclusion	**Situational crime prevention (SCP)** **Target hardening** to deal with the 'rational choice' to offend by reducing opportunities for crime, e.g. security guards, CCTV, gated communities
Wilson and Kelling and left realists agree that a lack of community and informal controls can lead to crime	**Community-based policing** The police must build better relationships with and be more accountable to the local community (e.g. police community support officers, or PCSOs, should work with local schools)	**Environmental crime prevention (ECP)** Wilson and Kelling (1982). 'Broken windows' must be replaced immediately. Zero tolerance policing on minor crimes will also help stop neighbourhood decline
Marxists would argue they both focus on street crime and ignore corporate crime	**Selective law enforcement** does exist, e.g. institutional racism occurs and policing needs to be improved	The police are professional and impartial and are an important part of the practical solution to reduce crime

Exam tip

You should link the 'broken windows' thesis to Hirschi's (1969) version of control theory, which argues that social bonds such as attachment hold society together and prevent people from committing crime. If minor crimes go unpunished, people will feel there is no social control in their community and start to feel detached from society, leading to crime.

Specific policies

SCP

The Port Authority Bus Terminal in New York was reshaped to 'design out' crime. For example, smaller sinks reduced the likelihood of the homeless using them to bathe (the aim of this was to reduce deviant activity such as rough sleeping).

Stoke Council introduced an improved street lighting scheme in one area, which reduced opportunities to commit street crime (crime was reduced by 26%).

ECP

In New York a **zero tolerance** policy of aggressive policing was adopted on minor crimes such as begging and fare dodging, and the Clean Car Program meant subway carriages with graffiti were immediately removed. The police proactively dealt with minor forms of disorder with the aim of preventing more serious crime.

SCCP

Sure Start aimed at tackling aspects of social exclusion by improving the educational opportunities of disadvantaged groups, such as working-class people and minority ethnic groups, and providing support for entering the labour market (such as preschool education and parenting classes).

The Perry Preschool project in the USA gave an intellectual enrichment programme to a selected group of disadvantaged black 3–4-year-olds for 2 years. By the age of 40, those who had followed the programme had lower rates of crime and were more likely to be in employment than their peers.

Evaluation

- ■ – While there is evidence that it can reduce certain types of crime by increasing the risks and effort of committing crime, a major criticism of SCP is **displacement**. Crime is not reduced, as criminals will rationally respond to target hardening by moving to where targets are softer. **Chaiken** et al. (1974) found that in New York a crackdown on subway robberies simply displaced them to the streets above.
- ■ + Evidence also suggests that ECP policies are effective. For example, in New York between 1993 and 1996 zero tolerance policies arguably led to a dramatic decline in most crimes (homicide rates fell by 50%).
- ■ – However, other reasons have been suggested for this reduction, such as a fall in unemployment, crack cocaine being less available, and the NYPD (City of New York Police Department) employing 7,000 extra officers.
- ■ – The zero tolerance policy of 'three strikes and you're out' has led to a dramatic increase in the prison population in the USA. High rates of recidivism (repeat offending) would suggest that tougher sentencing does not act as a deterrent and is not an effective policy of crime prevention.
- ■ – SCCP policies are often long-term solutions and it is difficult to measure their specific impact on crime reduction.
- ■ – Critics of left realist policies, such as right realists, argue that they are 'too soft' on criminals. They argue that individuals make rational choices to commit crimes and that crime is not caused by society.

Knowledge check 12

Outline two criticisms of ECP.

Exam tip

Be prepared to apply general evaluation points on the right realist and left realist theories of crime that these crime prevention strategies are based on (see the section on realist approaches to crime). For example, the criticism of the rational choice argument as being useless to explain crimes such as being drunk and disorderly would suggest that even SCP strategies such as CCTV or security guards would do little to prevent this crime.

Punishment and the role of prisons and surveillance

- Punishment, especially prison, is thought to reduce crime in the following ways:

  1 **Deterrence** Right realists argue that prison will increase the cost as against the benefit of crime, therefore deterring the criminal from making the rational choice to commit a crime.

  2 **Incapacitation** Right realists argue that prison is important as it removes the criminals from society so they cannot offend again.

  3 **Rehabilitation** Others see punishment such as prison as an opportunity to reform criminals through education and training so that they do not return to crime in the future.

- Functionalists such as **Durkheim** (1893) see the CJS as acting in the interests of society as a whole. He argues that public punishment of crimes is good for society because it leads to social solidarity and consensus as people come together to condemn the criminal. Durkheim felt that in traditional societies punishment tended to be based on **retributive justice**, which tends to be severe and based on revenge: 'an eye for an eye'. However, in a modern society punishment is more likely to be based on **restitutive justice** — aiming to restore the situation, such as by paying compensation to repair the damage caused by the crime.

- Marxists see punishment as serving the interests of capitalism by maintaining the existing capitalist social order and keeping the workers under control. **Althusser** (1971) argues that punishment is part of the **repressive state apparatus** that, along with the police and the CJS, is used to uphold the interests of the capitalist class, e.g. the protection of private property. Just like the law, Marxists would argue that punishment is selectively enforced. **Rusche and Kirchheimer** (1939) argue that as the interests of the ruling class change, so do the forms of punishment. The introduction of prisons was useful in early capitalism for training workers to the discipline of long hours in alienating and poor working conditions and to deal with periods of high unemployment.

- Despite New Labour's emphasis on being 'tough on the causes of crime', it agreed with the right realist approach of the Conservatives that there should be a strong emphasis on punishment. Subsequently, since the 1980s the UK prison population has steadily increased (from 60,000 in 1997 to 84,000 in 2019). **Garland** (2001) described the reliance on prisons as a form of punishment as an era of '**mass incarceration**'; in the USA this applied particularly to young black males. However, the high rates of **recidivism** (repeat offending) suggest that prison as a policy of crime control and prevention does not work. For the two thirds of prisoners who reoffend, prison clearly fails to act as a deterrent or perform the function of rehabilitation. Garland suggests that in the late-modern period the failure of such policies has led governments to be more concerned with creating the perception that they are managing rather than preventing crime (such as referring to official statistics that crime rates are falling).

- **Surveillance** as a form of social control and crime control has been expanding quietly for many decades and is now a growing feature of modern life. **Foucault** (1977) argues that the nature of social control (or discipline, as he refers to it) has changed from public punishments to the body, such as executions, to more subtle

Knowledge check 13

What did Foucault mean by disciplinary power?

forms of punishment, particularly in late modernity. As well as being carried out by a greater range of agents of social control than just the police, punishments now seek to control the mind as well as the body. Foucault argues that this **disciplinary power** is achieved though surveillance, which he felt was illustrated by the **panopticon** (meaning 'all-seeing place') whereby the design of the prison allowed guards to watch prisoners in their cells without being seen. This resulted in a form of **self-surveillance** — the prisoners would behave as they had no way of knowing whether the guards were watching them.

■ **Cohen** (1985) agreed with Foucault's idea that social control has now spread to more agents of social control, such as youth offending workers and even schools and private companies. Cohen (in Innes, 2003) argues that as a result of the increase in community-based controls such as antisocial behaviour orders (ASBOs), the CJS and the authorities have been able to cast the '**net of control**' over more people. Like Foucault, Cohen argues that this has led to the use of more subtle controls such as CCTV, electronic tagging and curfews. This links to the increased use of surveillance in crime control in the late-modern era.

Liquid surveillance

■ In the late-modern era, societies are more 'fluid' and their citizens, who are always on the move, are continually monitored, tracked and traced through CCTV, passwords and coded controls on buildings. **Bauman and Lyon** (2013) argue that this **liquid surveillance** is flexible and mobile and is spreading into more areas of life:

1 As travellers — passport control with body scanners and biometric checks, chips in passports, checking-in by smartphone

2 As consumers — strategies such as monitoring searches and cookies, customer databases, using smartphones to scan QR (quick response) codes or when purchasing goods

3 As users of social media — by exchanging personal information such as personal profiles

■ Whereas surveillance used to be solid and more fixed, such as in prisons, Bauman argues that it is now **post-panoptical**: the 'watchers' no longer need to be present and can escape beyond reach. While the details of our daily lives become more transparent to the organisations watching us, their activities become increasingly difficult to discern. In terms of social media, the loss of personal data to 'friends' illustrates how individual security may have to be sacrificed by individuals in order to partake in the 'cyberworld'.

■ Bauman and Lyon argue that the key metaphor for liquid surveillance is 'big brother' and that power can now move with the 'speed of an electrical button'. They argue that as well as privacy issues, liquid surveillance also involves issues of justice and human rights. They point to how 'Arabs and Muslims' are subjected to more 'random' security checks at airports than other groups. They also argue that the ever-increasing use of drone surveillance can be abused by powerful groups and nations, and provides no shelter for those spied upon.

Exam tip

Be prepared to link the topics of state crime and cybercrime to a question on social control, crime and surveillance. In terms of state crime, the use of drones in the 'war on terror' and air strikes in countries such as Syria are viewed by some as war crimes.

Victimisation

There are two main sociological theories that explain how people become victims of crime.

■ **Positivist victimology** As suggested by **Miers** (1989), positivist victimology focuses on interpersonal crimes of violence, attempts to identify the factors that produce patterns in victimisation and explains how victims have contributed to their own victimisation. In relation to the latter, factors which can lead to victimisation have been identified, for example low intelligence and actions such as being the first person to use violence. Positivist victimology has been criticised for victim blaming and for failing to examine less visible crime, such as state and green crime.

■ **Critical (or radical) victimology** This criticises positivist victimology for failing to take account of structural inequalities. **Mawby and Walklate** (1994) argue that victimisation is a form of structural powerlessness. Just as with crime, critical victimology argues that the idea of being a victim is socially constructed. **Christie** (1986) states that the stereotypical 'ideal victim' in society is generally weak, innocent and blameless and is the target of an attack by a stranger. Critical criminology points to how the CJS can deny a victim their status by not applying the label of victim. **Tombs and White** (2007) have pointed to the ideological nature of this. For example, by failing to press charges against employers for industrial injury, the crimes of capitalism remain hidden. Similarly, feminists argue that by not pressing charges in cases of domestic violence, the crime stays invisible and women are denied the status of victim and the right to any redress. Positivist victimology would criticise critical victimology for failing to acknowledge that victims bring their victimisation on themselves.

> **Knowledge check 14**
>
> Outline two criticisms of positivist victimology.

Patterns of victimisation

1 Men are almost twice as likely as women to become victims of violent crime, despite women having a greater fear of crime.

2 Women are more likely to be the victims of domestic violence and sexual attacks than men.

3 Young males aged between 16 and 24 experience most violent crime.

4 Minority ethnic groups, particularly those of mixed race, are more likely to be at risk of being a victim of crime than white people.

5 The poorest groups, such as unemployed people and homeless people, are more likely to be victims of crime than other social groups.

Summary

After studying this section, you should be aware of types of crime control, surveillance, prevention and punishment, victims, and the role of the criminal justice system and other agencies. You should be familiar with the following:

■ right and left realist crime prevention strategies

■ sociological explanations of the role of punishment, the criminal justice system and other agencies such as prisons

■ surveillance as a form of social and crime control, including liquid surveillance

■ positivist and critical victimology and patterns of victimisation

Theory and methods

For sociological research methods, which you will have studied in Year 1, refer to Student Guide 1, Education with theory and methods (see pages 27–42.)

■ Consensus, conflict, structural and social action theories

Functionalism

- Functionalism is a 'macro', large-scale structural theory that tends to use **positivist** methods to understand society and uncover the impact of social forces on individuals' behaviour. Durkheim (1897), who laid the foundations for modern functionalism, used a scientific approach to demonstrate how suicide was a social fact caused by factors external to the individual (see the section on sociology as a science).

- Parsons (1951) developed Durkheim's ideas into a systematic theory of society. The starting point is the **organic analogy**. Just like a living organism, society is made of **interconnected** and **interdependent** parts. Just as different parts of the body, such as the heart and brain, must work together to bring about good health, so different institutions, such as the family and the education system, must work together to bring about and maintain social order.

- Parsons argues that society has four basic needs (or **functional prerequisites**) that are met by four different **subsystems**:

  1 **Adaptation** Society has to provide a basic standard of living. Subsystem: economic, through institutions such as factories and the banking system.

  2 **Goal attainment** Society has to have decision-making procedures. Subsystem: political, through institutions such as political parties.

  3 **Integration** Society must develop institutions to ensure shared goals and reduce conflict. Subsystems: education, religion and the media.

  4 **Latency** Relates to how individuals are able to cope with society over time. Subsystem: kinship, through institutions such as the family. Parsons divides latency into **pattern maintenance**, such as families socialising their members into acceptable forms of behaviour and roles, and **tension management**, which ensures people are motivated to perform their roles and not oppose society.

- Functionalism argues that in order for the various parts of society to work together there must be **value consensus**. Basic norms and values, such as basic manners, are passed down through **primary socialisation** in the family, while agents of **secondary socialisation**, such as the education system, socialise children into the wider culture and the values of achievement and competition that are required in the workplace. In addition to socialisation, value consensus and social integration are also achieved though **social control**. This can occur through **informal agencies** of social control, for example the family using positive sanctions such as rewards, or through punishments administered by **formal agencies** of social control such as the criminal justice system.

- Both Durkheim and Parsons argue that industrialisation led to a change from a **traditional** to a **modern** society. Parsons argues that different **pattern variables** (typical patterns of norms) exist in each society. The pattern variables that existed in traditional societies, such as collective orientation and ascribed status (i.e. status fixed at birth), were replaced in a modern society by individualism and achieved status. However, functionalists believe that social change is **evolutionary**. Parsons argues that a process of **structural differentiation** occurs whereby institutions gradually develop to meet the needs of society. For example, in a modern society some of the functions performed by the kinship system, such as providing skills for future jobs, have been taken over by other institutions such as the education system.

Merton — an internal critique

- Merton (1957), a functionalist, argues that Parsons was wrong to assume that all institutions were functional for all parts of society. He argues that some institutions could be **dysfunctional** for society, such as religion leading to conflict and division in society. Merton also disagrees with Parsons' view that all institutions, such as the nuclear family, are **functionally indispensable**. He argues that there may be **functional alternatives**, such as same-sex parents being able to fulfil the function of effective socialisation. Merton feels that Parsons' analysis of society is too simplistic. For example, not all institutions are interdependent and there may be **latent** (hidden) functions as well as **manifest** (intended) ones.

Evaluation

- + Functionalism shows the macro influence of society over the individual.
- + Value consensus does exist in society. Different institutions do work together.
- − Functionalists such as Durkheim were not as scientific as is claimed. For example, he did not operationalise concepts such as integration in his study of suicide.
- − **Marxists** argue that functionalists ignore conflict and differences in power in society.
- − **Interactionists** and **postmodernists** argue that people are more reflexive (see page 36) and are not puppets whose actions are determined by pattern variables such as universalistic norms in schools (illustrated by students rejecting teacher labels).
- − **Postmodernism** regards functionalism as a **metanarrative** that cannot explain the diversity that exists in values in society today.
- − **Conflict theorists** and **postmodernists** would argue that functionalism overemphasises the level of consensus in society. For example, feminists claim that, as well as ignoring patriarchy, functionalists fail to explain differing attitudes towards gender roles in society today.
- − Functionalists' view of social change is criticised, particularly by **Marxists**, who argue that change can be revolutionary as well as evolutionary.

Exam tip

To illustrate general functionalist ideas, be prepared to refer to topic areas such as education and crime and deviance. For example, while Durkheim argued that the teaching of history would help develop social solidarity and a sense of belonging to society, Parsons thought that education acted as a bridge between the particularistic values of the home and the universalistic values of the workplace.

Marxism

- Like functionalism, Marxism is a macro, structural perspective that attempts to study the influence of social institutions over individuals in a scientific manner. Rather than it being based on consensus, however, Marx argued that capitalist society is based on conflict between two social classes, the **bourgeoisie** (Bs), who own the **means of production**, and the **proletariat** (Ps), the working class who hire out their labour in return for a wage. The Bs seek to maximise profits, or **surplus value**, by exploiting the Ps, leading to inequalities in income and wealth. Marx argued that this inequality would increase over time and lead to a **polarisation** of the classes, which would eventually lead to revolution.
- Marx argued that because the Bs owned the **infrastructure** (the economic base) of society, they were able to have control over other institutions in society contained in the **superstructure**, such as the family, religion, the media and the education system. The function of the superstructure was to pass on ruling-class ideology to the Ps and help **reproduce** and **legitimise** the inequalities that existed in a capitalist society. As a result, the Ps were lulled into a **false class consciousness** as they were 'brainwashed' into believing that capitalism was fair and were unable to see through the oppression they suffered. Marx argued that eventually the Ps would become a '**class for itself**' and wake up to the exploitation and inequality they faced, and would collectively overthrow capitalism and replace it with a classless **communist** society.
- Like Durkheim, Marx felt society should be studied in a scientific way. He described his theory as 'scientific socialism'. This can be seen in his theory of social change, referred to as **historical materialism**. He argued that the nature of class conflict and exploitation that exists between two social groups in every time period (epoch) changes over time. For example, in ancient society it was based on slavery, which changed to the ownership of land in the feudal period. Marx's 'hypothesis' was that after the proletariat revolution, there would be the establishment of the last epoch, communism, which would lead to an end to the exploitation and **alienation** that existed in capitalism.

> **Exam tip**
>
> Develop analysis by comparing the similarities and differences between functionalism and Marxism. For example, compare Marx's view that there are two key social institutions (with one, the infrastructure, controlling the other for the benefit of one group) with Parsons' view that there are four subsystems working harmoniously for the benefit of all society.

> **Exam tip**
>
> Be prepared to link other topics you have studied to explain the Marxist view of legitimation and reproduction. For example, discuss how Marxists Bowles and Gintis' concepts of the myth of meritocracy and the hidden curriculum can be used to examine class inequality in the education system. Similarly, the policy of the minimum wage would be viewed by Marxists as an ideological tool which justifies and legitimates low pay and exploitation while seemingly showing the caring face of capitalism.

Means of production The things required in the process of production that can be owned, such as land, machinery, tools and factories (but not labour).

Surplus value The difference between the value of goods produced and wages paid by capitalists.

Polarisation The process whereby, due to continued exploitation in capitalism, the rich will get richer and the poor will get poorer.

Historical materialism A methodological approach developed by Marx to study changes in how human societies collectively produce the necessities of life over time.

Alienation A feeling of a lack of control resulting from living in a society stratified into social classes. For example, on a factory assembly line, workers feel little job satisfaction due to a lack of input into the process of production.

Evaluation

- ■ + Marxism explains inequality in society. Workplace exploitation does occur.
- ■ + It shows how society, particularly economic factors, influences individuals.
- ■ + It provides an explanation for how conflict in society developed over time.
- ■ – **Functionalists** would argue that there is too much emphasis on conflict and that there are examples of capitalism benefiting all society, such as the welfare state and improvements in the standard of living. They argue that shared values do exist and that there is consensus in society.
- ■ – The revolution that Marx predicted has not occurred; capitalism has grown stronger and, as a result of globalisation, has spread across the world.
- ■ – When communist regimes have been established they have been unsuccessful, such as in China and the USSR. Marxists would counter this by arguing that they were not truly communist states.
- ■ – Class polarisation has not occurred. As **Weber** argues, the middle classes have grown considerably, contrary to Marx's prediction.
- ■ – **Feminists** argue that Marxists ignore gender inequality, such as the gender pay gap.
- ■ – **Social action theorists** argue that Marxism ignores the influence of the individual on society.

Neo-Marxism

- ■ Neo-Marxists **Althusser** and **Gramsci** (compared in Table 7) are critical of the economic determinism of traditional Marxism and both develop the theory of ideology. Gramsci, to an extent, adopts a micro, social action approach. He argues that individual ideas can exist independently of both the infrastructure and superstructure and that the Ps can to some extent see through the dominant ideology and can challenge the hegemony of the Bs.
- ■ Althusser adopts a macro, structural approach and argues that what will lead to social change is not people's actions but conflicts within the social structure, between economic, political and ideological levels. Althusser argues that there are two means through which the state reproduces capitalism: **repressive state apparatuses** (RSAs) such as the police and prisons, and **ideological state apparatuses** (ISAs) such as education and the media.

Hegemony The ideas and values of the ruling class that become the dominant view in society. These are transmitted via institutions such as the media, education and religion.

Table 7 A comparison of two neo-Marxist views

Gramsci — humanist		Althusser — structuralist
Humans have free will and are active. People's conscious ideas can lead to social change	Disagree	This is an illusion. Macro, structural factors will cause social change. People are puppets controlled by ideology
The working class can become class conscious and can see through dominant ideology	Disagree	This is a false consciousness constructed by ISAs — e.g. the myth of meritocracy in education
Working-class protests can lead to change — the proletariat can construct a counter-hegemonic bloc of leadership based on socialist principles	Disagree	The crisis in capitalism can lead to change as a result of contradictions between the three structures: economic, political and ideological
Coercion — force Ps to accept the rule of the Bs via police, the army and the courts	Agree	RSAs — these coerce the Ps to comply with the will of the Bs
Consent — the media, religion, education and so on persuade the Ps to accept the rule of the ruling class	Agree	ISAs — these ideologically manipulate the Ps to see capitalism as legitimate
Rejects economic determinism of Marx	Agree	Rejects economic determinism of Marx

- The term **the Frankfurt School** refers to other neo-Marxist sociologists who developed Marxist theory. Marcuse (1964) argues that Marx did not take account of the key role that the media play in shaping and manipulating our needs, e.g. through advertising. He argues that the media also divert the attention of the working class away from the injustices of capitalism by promoting trivial forms of entertainment, as seen in 'reality' television programmes today.

- A different type of neo-Marxism using a **postmodern** framework is developed by **Harvey** (1990). He argues that, since the 1970s, capitalism has moved into a different stage as a result of factors such as **globalisation** and the move in the economy from manufacturing to the service sector. This has led to what Harvey calls '**flexible accumulation**'. This involves new ways of achieving profits, such as exploiting the labour power in developing countries to produce cheap goods, requiring a more flexible workforce (e.g. through zero-hour contracts), and making technologically based products such as tablets and mobile phones. Harvey points to other effects of these changes on capitalism, such as transnational companies being more important than nation-states, and gender, ethnicity and religion replacing social class as the main forms of division and inequality in society.

Knowledge check 15

Outline two areas of agreement between Gramsci and Althusser.

Social action theory

- Social action theories reject structural, macro theories and argue that society is constructed through people's interactions and meanings (such as in the labelling process). Theories such as **symbolic interactionism** (the full name for interactionism) are micro, small-scale theories that tend to use interpretivist methods and reject the positivist approach adopted by structural theories. Social action theory argues that individuals, rather than being controlled like puppets by the nature of capitalist society (as Marxists argue) or pattern variables (as Parsons suggests), make their own choices and that society is constructed from people's meanings and interpretations. For example, while social roles such as teacher and student exist, they are only guidelines which individuals can interpret and negotiate with others.

- While accepting the significance of objective, causal, structural factors, **Weber** (1905) argued that the role of the sociologist was to uncover **verstehen** — the subjective meanings that individuals attach to their behaviour. He argued that interpretivist methods were needed to understand social action.

- **Symbolic interactionism** (SI) refers to the process whereby people acquire knowledge about what is appropriate behaviour in different social situations. **Mead** (1934) argued that the world is composed of many different symbols, which are not fixed but have meanings that shape our behaviour. For example, a kiss can be interpreted and responded to differently depending on the context in which it occurs. The response would differ greatly between the context of a first date and that of greeting a relative at a funeral.

- **Blumer** (1962) argues that as children we develop the notion of the **self**, which is partly due to how an individual interprets their experiences, such as learning social roles through playing games, but is also a product of how others see us. **Cooley** (1922) developed the idea of the **looking-glass self** to describe how we learn to see ourselves as others see us.

- Labelling theory developed from SI and was applied by **Becker** (1961) to study how agents of social control, such as teachers and the police, are able to apply negative labels in the process of interaction. These labels can have a negative impact on the self-esteem and status of those labelled, often leading to a **self-fulfilling prophecy** where the label is accepted (see page 9). **Goffman's** (1963) **dramaturgical** approach is a version of SI which argues that social interaction is like a play in which the roles of the 'actors' are only loosely 'scripted' by society.

- Unlike SI, which accepts the influence of the social structure, such as the influence of social class on educational achievement or offending, **phenomenologists** argue that society is not 'real' but socially constructed. In this view, social class is a phenomenon that is 'made up' by society. **Schutz** (1899–1959) argues that members of society use a set of shared categories or '**typifications**' to make sense of the world and clarify any meanings that are unclear. Schutz argues that these typifications or common-sense knowledge give the impression that the world is ordered but in fact it is socially constructed.

- These ideas were developed by **ethnomethodologist Garfinkel** (1967), who argued that rather than explaining the effects of meaning (such as the way coroners label deaths), sociologists should study the methods that are used to produce meanings in the first place, i.e. how actors create meanings. Garfinkel argues that we use **reflexivity** to make sense of the world when there is confusion over the meanings of certain behaviours. For example, coroners make sense of confusion over the cause of death by using their common-sense knowledge of 'facts' about suicide cases, such as the mental health of the deceased or their marital status.

- **Giddens** (1984) combines theories of structure and social action in his theory of **structuration**. He argues that while individuals are restricted by structural factors such as norms, customs and laws, they have choice and can respond to these factors in different ways. Giddens argues that increasingly in a late-modern society, social structures are open to change by the actions of individuals.

Evaluation

- + Social action theory, with its emphasis on interpretivist methodology, has provided a rich insight into the interaction process in small-scale settings.
- + Social action theories are voluntaristic — they demonstrate how people have free will and are able to shape society.
- + Social action theories such as interactionism avoid the deterministic nature of structural theories such as Marxism and functionalism.
- – **Structural theories** argue that social action theory fails to take account of the wider social context in which interaction takes place. It fails to explain the origins of labels and symbolic meanings.
- – **Functionalists** argue that social action theory ignores the influence of consistent patterns, such as shared norms, on people's behaviour. Ethnomethodology, in particular, has been criticised for denying the existence of a wider society.
- – **Marxists** and **feminists** argue that social action theory fails to fully explore power differences between individuals and social groups. In response, Becker argues that labelling theory does examine the power relationship between those labelled and the agents of social control.
- – Giddens' structuration theory has been criticised by **Marxists** for overestimating the extent to which individuals can change social structures.

Exam tip

Be prepared to discuss the differences between the various social action approaches. While labelling theory has been criticised for seeing the individual as passively accepting labels, Goffman argues that, through impression management, individuals actively seek to present themselves in a way they wish others to see them.

Reflexivity The use of common-sense knowledge to make sense of social reality.

Exam tip

Be prepared to apply the ideas of Garfinkel and phenomenologists such as Atkinson (see page 43) to the debate as to whether sociology is a science. They totally reject Durkheim's positivist, scientific approach and argue that the official statistics that are used to explain suicide are socially constructed. They would argue that these statistics tell us more about the common-sense assumptions of coroners and cannot be used to make 'laws' about the causes of suicide.

Feminism

Knowledge check 16

What is the difference between phenomenology and symbolic interactionism?

Like Marxism, feminism is a conflict theory that tends to adopt a structuralist approach. However, feminists argue that inequalities are based on **patriarchy**, or male dominance, rather than on social class. Feminism seeks to show how social institutions such as the family, education and the media can contribute to the oppression of women. While quantitative data would be used to show structural patterns of gender inequality, such as the pay gap, most feminist research is qualitative and interpretivist in nature. For example, **Dobash and Dobash** (1979) used informal, unstructured interviews to gain an understanding of the experiences of women who had been the victims of domestic violence. Feminism is critical of traditional sociology for being **malestream**, as it ignores the viewpoint of women. There are three main types of feminist theory (see Table 8).

Table 8 Feminist theories

	Liberal feminism (LF) — Oakley (1974)	Marxist feminism (MF) — Barrett (1980)	Radical feminism (RF) — Firestone (1972)
What is the problem?	Lack of opportunities in education, employment and politics. Women's oppression has been maintained through sexist **gender socialisation** — e.g. the belief that the housewife–mother role is the primary role for women	Patriarchal **capitalism** controls and exploits women: ■ the unpaid role of housewife, which nurtures the current and next generation of workers ■ absorbing the anger of male workers, e.g. domestic violence ■ part of the **reserve army of labour**	Men are the 'enemy'. **Patriarchy** exists in all areas of society. Due to childbirth, women are dependent on men, who oppress and exploit them in all areas of life, from sexual relations in the home to discrimination in the workplace
How should it be solved?	By changing socialisation patterns, e.g. by having positive female role models in the media. Through legislation such as the Equal Pay Act. LFs argue that the **feminisation** of education and the economy provides evidence that women's opportunities are improving	Capitalism must be overthrown for women to be free from oppression and patriarchy. It is the main cause of women's oppression. Barrett argues that the ideology of '**familism**' must also be overthrown. This promotes to women the idea that they should accept and be satisfied with their role as housewife–mother within the nuclear family	Revolutionary change: ■ **Separation** Some RFs argue that women must live separately from men to break free from male violence and sexual aggression ■ **Political lesbianism** Other RFs argue that lesbianism is the only way in which women can escape male oppression in relationships
Strengths	LFs are arguably correct that changes in gender socialisation and legislation have reduced inequality	MFs are right to draw attention to the impact of capitalism on gender inequality. As well as the pay gap, males dominate the top positions in the economy	RF has demonstrated how female oppression occurs in the private sphere of domestic and sexual relationships
Weaknesses	MF and RF would argue that LF exaggerates progress and ignores the continuing influence of capitalism and patriarchy on gender inequality. The Equal Pay Act has not led to equal pay	Not all women are part of a reserve army of labour. This theory also fails to explain why some jobs are dominated by women or why women do most domestic labour. MF fails to explain gender inequality in non-capitalist societies	RF has been criticised for being too extreme. Its solutions of separation and political lesbianism are unrealistic. MF argues that class and not patriarchy is the real cause of women's oppression

Reserve army of labour A Marxist concept to explain how groups, such as women, can be brought into the labour market when there is a shortage of workers. When there is a boom in a capitalist economy they will be hired; when there is a recession they will be the first to be fired.

Further evaluation points on feminist theories

- Liberal feminists would argue that Marxist feminists and radical feminists fail to recognise how women's position has improved as a result of changes in legislation and attitudes to gender roles.
- **Dual systems** feminists such as Hartman (1979) criticise Marxist feminism and liberal feminism for being too simplistic and argue that capitalism and patriarchy are intertwined to form '**patriarchal capitalism**'.
- Due to its structural nature, feminism can be accused of being over-deterministic. It does not take account of how individual females may interpret their situation. As **Hakim** (2000) argues, not all women feel oppressed by being housewives and mothers.
- **Difference feminists** would argue that theories such as liberal feminism which argue that patriarchy is universal are failing to acknowledge that women are not a homogeneous group. The experiences of women will be influenced by a range of factors such as social class, ethnicity, religion and age.
- **Black feminists** agree and argue that forms of feminism that strive to overcome patriarchy and class oppression but ignore ethnicity can discriminate against women through racial bias.
- **Postmodern feminists** also agree that previous feminist theories fail to reflect the diversity of the experiences of women and that issues such as patriarchy do not affect all women in the same way. Like all modern theorists, postmodernists regard feminism as a metanarrative.

Exam tip

If you are asked to evaluate the usefulness of feminist theories in understanding society, be prepared to discuss the strengths and weaknesses of the different types of feminism. When evaluating feminist theories, you should also refer to how they relate to other sociological theories, e.g. the agreement between Marxism and Marxist feminists.

Exam tip

As well as the methodological approach used by feminists, be prepared to link topic areas to a question on feminism, such as improvement in educational achievement to support the liberal feminist view or the use of 'sex to sell' in gender portrayal in the media to support the Marxist feminist arguments.

■ Modernity and postmodernism

- The industrial revolution which led to urbanisation, capitalism and the development of nation-states led to the start of modernity, or modern society. **Modern theories** such as Marxism, functionalism and positivism were part of the **Enlightenment project** — the belief that knowledge and rational, scientific thinking could lead to progress in society. For example, positivist sociology rejected traditional sources of knowledge such as religion and argued that a scientific approach was needed to explain how the modern world worked and could be improved.
- **Postmodernists** argue, however, that the rapid social and economic changes that occurred in the later part of the twentieth century (from around the late 1970s) have led to the end of the modern era. Significant aspects of a postmodern society, often based on globalisation, include:

1   A shift from **Fordist** mass production to a **post-Fordist** economy based on the service sector, technology and the need for a flexible workforce.

2   The decline of traditional sources of identity, particularly social class. These have been replaced by the consumption of consumer goods, notably global brands such as Nike and Apple.

3   Life in a media-saturated society where popular culture shapes personal identity through satellite television and, increasingly, the internet and mobile phones.

■ Postmodernist **Lyotard** (1984) argues that contemporary society cannot be explained by metanarratives, such as Marxism and functionalism, as it is based on isolated individuals who are linked by a few social bonds, rather than being controlled by structural factors.

■ **Baudrillard** (1983) agrees that individuals are largely isolated and argues that the increasing consumption of the media to experience the world has led to the '**death of the social**'. He also argues that we consume commodities as a sign or way of expressing ourselves rather than for the function that they perform. He develops the idea of **simulacra**, meaning that media images that are not based on reality, such as 'celebrities', are increasingly used to model our behaviour. The media also create a world of **hyperreality**, where people cannot distinguish image from reality (e.g. the belief that 'celebrities' such as Keith Lemon are real).

■ Rather than society moving to a new set of economic and social circumstances as postmodernists argue, **late modernists** see the rapid social changes that have recently occurred as a continuation of modern society. Late-modernist theorists such as **Giddens** (1984) and **Beck** (1992) agree with postmodernists that factors such as increasing individualism and globalisation are causing new problems for society. However, they share the view of the Enlightenment project that these problems can be addressed and that reason can be used to improve society.

■ Giddens' **structuration theory** (see the section on social action theory) claims that there is a **duality of structure** — that people (or 'agents', as Giddens calls them) can 'make' society as well as being influenced by it. Giddens argues that people engage in **reflexivity** (see page 36), whereby they constantly monitor their own situation in the light of information and seek change if needed.

■ Beck agrees with Giddens and argues that the complex changes of the late-modern period, such as global warming and an unstable economy, have led to what he calls a **risk society**. He argues that individuals are more aware of these ever-increasing risks and use reflexivity to take action to reduce them. This can range from joining political movements such as the 'War on Poverty' or improving lifestyles by changing eating habits.

Exam tip

Be prepared to compare Giddens' use of reflexivity with social action theory. Giddens develops the symbolic interactionist notion of taking the role of the other as, through reflexivity, individuals are able to see themselves as others see them and create their own identity. Ethnomethodologists argue that reflexivity is not just used to shape our own identities but is used to make sense of reality and social order itself.

Exam tip

In evaluating the postmodern and late-modern views, be prepared to discuss the views of Harvey and the Marxist version of how capitalism has developed after the modern era (see the neo-Marxism section).

Evaluation

- ■ + Late modernists and postmodernists are right to draw attention to the inadequacies of modern theories in explaining recent changes in society, such as the impact of globalisation.
- ■ + Postmodernists are right to argue that there is greater diversity and choice in society and people are able to 'pick and mix' their own identity via the media and the consumption of cultural products.
- ■ − **Modern theories** would argue that the ability to make these choices and consume is dependent on factors such as social class, gender and ethnicity.
- ■ − **Conflict theories** criticise postmodernists for ignoring the significance of structural factors and how gender and class shape people's life chances and identity.
- ■ − **Social action theory** argues that postmodernism ignores interactions between individuals and that people are active and able to distinguish between fiction and reality.
- ■ − Postmodernism is critical of sociological theories for not offering the 'truth' — but why should we accept their view of society as accurate?
- ■ − Beck has been criticised for ignoring the fact that the risks faced may be influenced by factors such as social class and that some individuals may not have the power to use reflexivity to reduce these risks.
- ■ − Postmodernists reject the view of late modernists that the 'risks' of society can be reduced by reflexivity.

Knowledge check 17

Outline two strengths of postmodern theory.

■ The relationship between sociological theory and methods

Figure 1 provides an overview of the relationship between theory and methods. *Refer to Student Guide 1, Education with theory and methods for sociological research methods (pages 27–42).*

While Figure 1 provides a useful outline of the link between theory and method, it is to a certain extent artificial, as researchers' choice of method may be influenced by a variety of factors, including practical and ethical issues. For example, consider a researcher carrying out a **longitudinal study**. Rather than being a specific type of method, this is a study where the researcher follows the same sample over an extended period and conducts research at set intervals (e.g. every five years). Within this type of study, a **positivist** would favour the use of questionnaires to gain statistics so correlations over time could be measured and causes identified. In contrast, an **interpretivist** would value longitudinal research for providing more than just a one-off snapshot and would favour the use of unstructured interviews to examine developments over time. However, for both types of approach a researcher would face some practical problems of longitudinal research. It is costly, takes time to get results and faces sample attrition — people may drop out of the study, so the sample may become less representative.

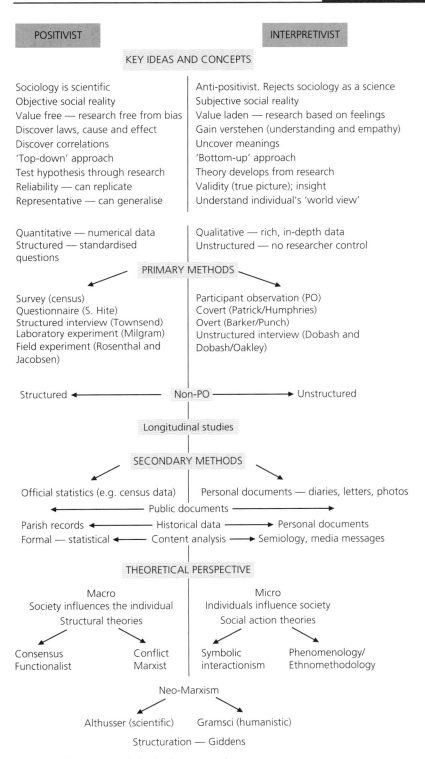

POSITIVIST | INTERPRETIVIST

KEY IDEAS AND CONCEPTS

Positivist	Interpretivist
Sociology is scientific	Anti-positivist. Rejects sociology as a science
Objective social reality	Subjective social reality
Value free — research free from bias	Value laden — research based on feelings
Discover laws, cause and effect	Gain verstehen (understanding and empathy)
Discover correlations	Uncover meanings
'Top-down' approach	'Bottom-up' approach
Test hypothesis through research	Theory develops from research
Reliability — can replicate	Validity (true picture); insight
Representative — can generalise	Understand individual's 'world view'

Quantitative — numerical data	Qualitative — rich, in-depth data
Structured — standardised questions	Unstructured — no researcher control

PRIMARY METHODS

Survey (census)	Participant observation (PO)
Questionnaire (S. Hite)	Covert (Patrick/Humphries)
Structured interview (Townsend)	Overt (Barker/Punch)
Laboratory experiment (Milgram)	Unstructured interview (Dobash and
Field experiment (Rosenthal and Jacobsen)	Dobash/Oakley)

Structured ← Non-PO → Unstructured

Longitudinal studies

SECONDARY METHODS

Official statistics (e.g. census data)	Personal documents — diaries, letters, photos

← Public documents →

Parish records ← Historical data → Personal documents

Formal — statistical ← Content analysis → Semiology, media messages

THEORETICAL PERSPECTIVE

Macro	Micro
Society influences the individual	Individuals influence society
Structural theories	Social action theories

Consensus Functionalist	Conflict Marxist	Symbolic interactionism	Phenomenology/ Ethnomethodology

Neo-Marxism

Althusser (scientific) Gramsci (humanistic)

Structuration — Giddens

Figure 1 Two methodological perspectives

Summary

After studying these sections, you should be aware of consensus, conflict, structural and social action theories, the concepts of modernity and postmodernity in relation to sociological theory, and the relationship between theory and methods. You should be familiar with the following:

- the difference between consensus theories, e.g. functionalism, and conflict theories, e.g. different Marxist and feminist theories
- the difference between structural theories, e.g. functionalism and Marxism, and action theories, e.g. symbolic interactionism, phenomenology and ethnomethodology
- attempts to combine structural and action theories such as structuration and humanist neo-Marxism
- modern, late-modern and postmodern theories of contemporary society
- the relationship between methodological approaches of positivism and interpretivism and sociological theory

Sociology as a science

Positivism versus interpretivism

- Positivists such as **Durkheim** argue that sociology can and should model itself on the natural sciences and use quantitative methods to study society objectively.
- Positivists argue that sociologists can discover laws about human behaviour by using the **hypothetico-deductive model**. This goes through the following stages: the researcher observes something, thinks of a hypothesis to explain it, gathers data through systematic observation and measurement, and establishes a law to show how the evidence supports the hypothesis. The process of **verification**, checking that something is true, should be used to prove or refute a hypothesis.
- Positivists believe that, as it is possible for sociologists to study social phenomena objectively, value freedom is possible as the researcher's own beliefs will not influence how they conduct their research or interpret their results.
- Durkheim used the **comparative method**, comparing suicide statistics to discover laws of cause and effect for suicide. He believed that patterns in suicide rates were caused by differences in social integration and moral regulation. Having examined, for different European countries, correlations between suicide rates and other variables such as religion, he argued that suicide rates were social facts, caused by the structure of the society, and were external to the individual.
- **Gibbs and Martin** argue that Durkheim was not scientific as he did not operationalise concepts such as social integration.
- Interpretivists and social action theorists reject the claim that sociology can be a science. They argue that the purpose of sociological inquiry is to uncover meanings and gain verstehen through qualitative methods, not to establish cause and effect. They would argue that sociologists, rather than being value free and objective, need to be subjective and will inevitably be influenced by their values.

- Interactionist **Douglas** (1967) rejects Durkheim's use of official statistics to make laws on suicide. Douglas argues that suicide statistics, rather than being scientific and objective, are based on the subjective opinions of coroners. Their verdicts may be influenced by factors such as relatives not wanting a suicide verdict to bring shame on their family, particularly in a Catholic country.
- Ethnomethodologist **Atkinson** (1978) argues that suicide is an individual act, not a social fact. Official statistics on suicide are socially constructed — they say more about the interpretations of coroners than levels of suicide. Interactionists believe that by using a '**bottom-up**' approach, sociologists can develop theories such as labelling being based on 'macro' factors such as social class. However, ethnomethodologists totally reject causal explanations of human behaviour. They argue that there are no macro, structural explanations for social phenomena that can be studied in a scientific way as positivists suggest.

Views on the nature of science

- **Popper** rejects the hypothetico-deductive approach of positivism and argues that scientific knowledge should be based on the process of **falsification** (proving something wrong) rather than verification. Therefore a hypothesis should be something that can be proved wrong. Popper feels that while sociology could be scientific, as it can produce a hypothesis that can be tested, most sociology is unscientific as it cannot be proved wrong (e.g. Marx's 'hypothesis' of communism).
- **Kuhn** (1962) argues that scientific knowledge works within a shared framework agreed by members, which he refers to as a **paradigm**. He rejects the views of science held by positivists and Popper and argues that there is no objective independent scientific knowledge. Rather, scientific knowledge works within paradigms, such as the view that the Earth is flat, which will only change when enough evidence is found that is not supported by the paradigm. Kuhn argues that as sociology does not have a shared and dominant paradigm, due to various competing theories, it cannot be considered to be a science.
- **Feyerabend** (1975) is also critical of positivists and Popper and argues that individual scientists will bend the rules and 'tweak' data to prove their theories, rather than being objective and rational. There have been many examples of 'cheating' in science, such as Burt's research into three types of intelligence which formed the basis for the tripartite education system.
- **Realists** argue that like some natural scientists, such as meteorologists, sociologists have to study society in '**open systems**', where variables cannot necessarily be controlled and measured. Therefore, sociology can attempt to be scientific in studying open systems in a neutral way. Just like some natural sciences, sociology studies unobservable, underlying structures. For example, social class cannot be directly observed, but its impact, such as on educational attainment, can be measured.
- There are therefore four main views on science:
  1 Positivist — prove theories by testing a hypothesis — verification
  2 Popper — prove other theories wrong — falsification
  3 Kuhn — scientific knowledge is based on paradigms — which offer explanations
  4 Realist — science studies open and closed systems — science is about the search for underlying causes of things

Knowledge check 18

What is the difference between the views of Popper and the positivist view of science?

- **Postmodernists** such as **Lyotard** (1992) reject the idea of absolute truths and objectivity in knowledge. They argue that all knowledge is relative and that the view of science is just one version of 'the truth'. Postmodernists regard 'modern', positivist theories such as functionalism and Marxism as '**metanarratives**' ('big stories') that do not hold 'the truth' about society. They are out of date as they are no longer able to explain the diverse and fragmented nature of postmodern society.
- Postmodernism is criticised for being contradictory. Why should we believe postmodernism's version of 'the truth'?
- Similarly, some **feminists** argue that sociology should not attempt to be scientific. While some argue that no single scientific feminist theory could explain the experiences of all women, others argue that qualitative methods need to be used to gain understanding of the experiences of women.

Exam tip

Be prepared to apply issues from the sociology as a science debate as to whether sociology can be value free. For example, realists argue that sociology can attempt to be scientific in studying open systems in a neutral way but they argue that sociologists cannot be completely value free.

Objectivity and values in sociology

- **Classical positivists** such as **Durkheim** argued that sociology could be value free. Sociologists should discover laws about human behaviour in order to understand how society works and to improve it through social policies. Positivists believe it is the job of the sociologist to establish 'the truth' in a neutral, detached way. Value freedom is possible as the researcher's own beliefs should not influence how they conduct their research or interpret their results.
- **Interpretivists** and social action theorists reject the claim that sociology can be value free and objective. They argue that sociologists aim to uncover meanings and gain verstehen using qualitative methods. They would argue that sociologists need to be subjective and will inevitably be influenced by their values.
- **Weber** argues that sociologists cannot be value free in three of the four stages of research he identifies: when choosing a research topic (Stage 1), interpreting research findings (Stage 3) and applying findings (Stage 4). However, he feels that researchers should be objective and unbiased in the second stage of research, that of carrying out their research.
- Modern positivists argue that sociologists can be value free as they can and should remain morally neutral when conducting research. Many sociologists such as Weber and **Gouldner** reject this view. They argue that as citizens, researchers have a '**moral responsibility**' and cannot divorce themselves from the potential harm that could result from their research findings.
- Gouldner also argues that sociologists should be 'committed' rather than 'morally neutral' and pretending to be value free. Sociologists such as **Marxists** and **feminists** argue that value freedom is undesirable and that sociologists should be **value laden** — they should make value judgements and should aim to improve society through sociological research.

Exam tip

An exam question may ask you to evaluate the claim that sociology can and/or should be value free. Make sure that arguments and evaluation points are clearly applied to these different claims.

- **Labelling theorist Becker** argues that sociologists should take the side of the 'underdog', such as working-class students and criminals labelled by powerful groups in society. Becker feels that interpretivist methods should be used to gain verstehen on the view of the 'outsiders'. Gouldner is critical of this as not going far enough. As a Marxist he argues that sociologists should be on the side of the people fighting back against capitalist society. This illustrates how both the theoretical and methodological perspectives that a sociologist chooses to adopt will reflect their values, which argues against the notion that sociology can be value free (see Figure 1 on page 41).

- For **postmodernists** all knowledge is relative; no one theory holds the absolute objective truth. All modern theories, such as Marxism and functionalism, are metanarratives and are based on values and assumptions. However, postmodernism could itself be described as a metanarrative.

- Other factors may mean that sociologists cannot be value free in their research, such as who funds the research (e.g. governments may not publish findings they disagree with) and the sociologists' own careers (they may choose to study a popular topic that could further their career).

Summary

After studying these sections, you should be aware of the nature of science and the extent to which sociology can be regarded as scientific, and debates about subjectivity, objectivity and value freedom. You should be familiar with the following:

- debates about the scientific status of sociology: positivist and interpretivist views
- different views of the natural sciences, e.g. positivism, Popper, Kuhn and realism, and implications for sociology's scientific status
- postmodern and feminist views on sociology as a science
- different views on whether sociology can and should be objective or value free, e.g. classical sociology, value neutrality and committed sociology

Exam tip

Be prepared to relate methodological issues to the question of objectivity and value freedom. Interpretivist methods such as participant observation can lose objectivity if the researcher 'goes native', while in 'objective' positivist methods such as questionnaires the researcher has imposed their own values on respondents by having predetermined questions.

Knowledge check 19

What is the difference between value free and value laden?

■ Sociology and social policy

Worsley (1977) described a **social** problem as social behaviour such as juvenile delinquency that causes public and private misery and that requires a collective response, whereas a **sociological** problem is any pattern of behaviour that requires explanation. A sociological problem could be a social problem or 'normal' behaviour such as conforming to laws.

Social policies are parts of government policies that attempt to deal with social problems such as educational underachievement and crime. Social policy has been influenced by sociological perspectives and research in a variety of ways:

- In line with the Enlightenment project, **positivists** such as **Comte** and **Durkheim** saw sociological research as being crucial in combating social problems and improving society through rational thought. **Functionalists** agree and argue that the role of the sociologist is to provide the government with objective research findings based on positivist methodology. They argue that this information, such as research on educational achievement, can be used to inform social policies that will serve the interests of society as a whole.

- The **social democratic** perspective had a significant impact on the introduction of the welfare state after the Second World War. Later, Townsend's *Poverty in the United Kingdom* (1979) made recommendations to the government to change what he felt was an inadequate benefits system.

- Whereas the social democratic view argues that the state should redistribute wealth and income, the **New Right** view is that the state should have only a minimal involvement in society and that social policy can be the cause of social problems such as poverty. Researchers such as Marsland and his notion of the **dependency culture** influenced Conservative governments to cut back on welfare provision in the 1980s and beyond.

- Feminist theory and research have influenced government policies aimed at addressing gender inequality such as the GIST (Girls into Science and Technology) project in education and the Equal Pay Act. Whereas **liberal feminists** would argue that such policies have improved the status of women in society, **radical feminists** believe that they have had little impact and that until patriarchy has been removed, inequalities such as the gender pay gap will continue. **Marxist feminists** would also be critical of much social policy, arguing that it oppresses women and undervalues their labour in both the workplace and the home.

- Many **Marxists** are critical of government social policies and argue that they can be used by the capitalist system to maintain and justify inequality. For example, they would argue that the minimum wage legitimises exploitation in the labour market while giving the impression to the public that government is acting in the best interests of the low paid. While some Marxists acknowledge that some social policies have benefited the working class, they believe the role of sociological research is to highlight the inequalities of capitalism rather than to inform social policy.

- Despite the influence of sociological research on social policy, governments may reject or not make use of research findings for a variety of reasons, particularly cost, their own political standpoint and electoral popularity. The social policies of governments will also be influenced by pressure groups such as the Confederation of British Industry (CBI) and global interests such as the EU.

Exam tip

An exam question may simply ask you to refer to the link between sociology and social policy. In addition to outlining the influence of sociological theory and research on social policy, and factors that act against this influence, you should also refer to the debate over whether it is the role of sociologists to inform social policy.

Summary

After studying this section, you should be aware of the relationship between sociology and social policy. You should be familiar with the following:
- the difference between social problems and sociological problems
- perspectives on social policy and the role of sociology in relation to policy

Knowledge check 20

What factors may prevent sociological research from influencing a government's social policy?

Questions & Answers

■ How to use this section

Following this introduction, this section of the guide contains three test papers on **Crime and deviance with theory and methods** in the style of the questions you can expect in the A-level Paper 3 examination. The content, timings and mark allocation of these papers are shown below.

The questions are followed by a brief analysis of what to watch out for when answering them. An A*-grade response to each question is given, with commentary explaining where marks are gained or lost. The A*-grade responses represent one way of achieving an A* grade. However, there is no such thing as a perfect essay. An A* grade can be achieved in a number of different ways. The advice below offers some suggestions on how this can be achieved.

The information in this guide can be used for the following exam papers:

Paper 3 Crime and deviance with theory and methods

The exam paper is allocated 2 hours.
- **Crime and deviance** Short answers (4- and 6-mark questions) and extended writing (10- and 30-mark questions). 50 marks
- **Theory and methods** Extended writing (10- and 20-mark questions). 30 marks

Paper 1 Education with theory and methods

- **Theory and methods** Extended writing (10-mark question). 10 marks

There is also a 10-mark 'Outline and explain' question on Paper 1 on Theory and methods, so the questions in this guide will be useful practice for this exam as well. The Content Guidance section in this guide, particularly the material on sociological theory, can be used to help prepare for the 10-mark essay question in this paper (refer to Student Guide 1, Education with theory and methods, for practice papers for the 10-mark questions on Theory and methods and for a more detailed coverage of sociological methods).

> The extended writing questions for 20 and 30 marks will make a specific reference to an 'item'. You should always make use of the item but should never copy out material from it. Try to refer to it and use it to make your own point in your own words. However, for the 10-mark 'apply' question it is essential to quote the item.

Examinable skills

AQA Sociology examination papers are designed to test certain defined skills. These skills are expressed as assessment objectives (AOs). There are three AOs and it is important that you know what these are and what you have to be able to do in an exam to show your ability in each. Further guidance on each of the AOs is given below. In practice, many answers to questions, particularly those carrying the higher marks, will contain elements of all three AOs.

Assessment objective 1 (AO1)

Demonstrate knowledge and understanding of:

- **sociological theories, concepts and evidence**
- **sociological research methods**

Your exam answers will have to demonstrate clearly to the examiners that your knowledge is accurate and appropriate to the topic being discussed and that you have a clear understanding of it. It is not enough simply to reproduce knowledge learned by rote. You must be able to use this knowledge in a meaningful way to answer the specific question set. This means that you must be able to *select* the appropriate knowledge from everything you know and use only the knowledge that is relevant to, and addresses the issues raised by, the question.

Assessment objective 2 (AO2)

Apply sociological theories, concepts, evidence and research methods to a range of issues.

In certain questions in the exam you will be presented with an item — a short paragraph setting the context for the question that is to follow and providing you with some information to help answer it. You *must* take this relevant information and use (apply) it in your answer. However, 'applying' the material does not mean simply copying it from the item and leaving it to speak for itself. You will need to show your understanding of the material by doing something with it, such as offering a criticism, explaining something about it, linking it to a particular sociological theory or offering another example of what is being stated or suggested. You will therefore be using your own knowledge to add to the information that you have been given and will be *applying* it appropriately to answer the question. (See the specific guidance below on using the item for Q03.)

Assessment objective 3 (AO3)

Analyse and evaluate sociological theories, concepts, evidence and research methods in order to:

- **present arguments**
- **make judgements**
- **draw conclusions**

The skill of *analysis* is shown by breaking something down into its component parts and subjecting them to detailed examination. Analysis is shown by providing answers (depending, of course, on what you are analysing) to questions such as 'who said or who believes this?', 'what does this concept relate to?', 'what does this research method entail?', 'how was this evidence collected?' and so on. The skill of *evaluation* is shown by the ability to identify the strengths and weaknesses or limitations of any sociological material. It is not sufficient, however, simply to list the strengths or limitations of something — you need to say *why* something is considered a strength or otherwise, and sometimes you will need to state *who* claims that this is a strength or weakness. Depending on what you are discussing, you may be able to reach a conclusion about the relative merits or otherwise of something, but remember that any conclusions should be based on the rational arguments and solid sociological evidence that you have presented in your answer.

Weighting of assessment objectives

In the exam papers, each AO is given a particular weighting, which indicates its relative importance to the overall mark gained.

Table 9 Weighting for A-level examinations

Assessment objective	Paper 1 (%)	Paper 2 (%)	Paper 3 (%)	Overall weighting (%)
AO1	15	13	16	44
AO2	11	11	9	31
AO3	8	9	8	25
Overall	33.33	33.33	33.33	100

Command words

It is important to take time in an exam to read the questions carefully before you start writing. Ofqual, the body that sets the criteria for all GCE sociology specifications, has an approved list of 'command words' that are used in exam questions. It is worth learning what is meant by these command words, to ensure that you give an appropriate response. Below is an explanation of the ones used for the questions on Paper 3 (and Paper 1).

Outline — give the main characteristics.

Outline and explain — give the main characteristics and develop these.

Analyse — separate information into components and identify their characteristics.

Evaluate —make judgements from the available evidence.

Applying material from the item — draw on the material provided and develop it using your own knowledge to answer the question. (Remember to make use of the item, but not to copy from it.)

Guidance on how to complete each question

Question 01

Outline two…

Here is an example:

Outline two criticisms of the use of situational crime prevention strategies to reduce crime (4 marks; see page 81).

Each point will be rewarded as 2 marks (1 + 1). You *must* link your explanation to the key words in the question. In this example 1 mark will be given for identifying a criticism (such as 'displacement') and 1 mark for the explanation of how this affects crime reduction (such as that if street lights are made brighter in one area of a town, crime will simply move to an adjacent area where the lights are less bright).

Question 02

Outline three…

Here is an example:

Outline three ways in which the media may cause crime (6 marks; see page 81).

Each point will be rewarded as 2 marks (1 + 1). You *must* link your explanation to the key words in the question. In this example 1 mark will be given for identifying a factor (such as moral panics) and 1 mark for the explanation of how this may cause crime (such as how sensationalised media reporting of youth subcultures may lead to youths wanting to join gangs and commit crimes such as fighting).

> It may be worth including an extra point for Questions 01 and 02 as the examiner will mark all the responses given and select the best ones. It is advisable to return to these questions and give an additional point if you have completed your answers before the end of the exam.

Question 03

Applying material from Item A, analyse two…

Here is an example:

Applying material from Item A, analyse two reasons that may influence whether females commit crime (10 marks; see page 56).

Remember you only need two paragraphs. No introduction or conclusion is required.

> Be concise on Questions 01 and 02. You can use bullet points and should not need to write more than two sentences for each point.

The first paragraph for the question above could be set out as follows:

- First sentence: Quote the 'hook' from the item. For this question, the first sentence could be as follows: 'The first reason that may influence whether females commit crime is because "females are controlled in various areas of society".'
- AO1: **Explain** — Outline what this means and give some examples to illustrate. For this question, for instance, you could give examples of how females may be controlled in the home or the workplace.
- AO3: **Analyse** — Unpack this with a discussion of the 'reason'. For this question, for instance, you could discuss how females are controlled in different areas of society according to feminists such as Heidensohn or Carlen.
- AO2: **Apply** — Explain why this 'reason' may influence whether females commit crime (apply points clearly to the question).
- AO3: **Evaluation** — Include at least one sentence starting with the word 'However'. For this question, the feminist view of control theory could be evaluated by arguments that this approach portrays females as passive victims of social control.

> In order to gain good application marks for Q03, it is a good strategy to use the exact words of the question in your response (such as 'way', 'reason' or 'effect').

The same structure should be used for paragraph two, which should quote a second hook in Item A — in this question, the reference to 'society becoming less patriarchal' or to 'women adopting more traditionally male attitudes and behaviours' (see page 55).

In addition to 'reasons', other words typically used in Question 03 are 'ways' or 'effects' (i.e. 'analyse two ways' or 'analyse two effects').

> In order to gain good marks for evaluation, points should be explicitly applied to the question. General evaluation points will not score as well.

Question 04

Applying material from Item B and your knowledge, evaluate…

Here is an example:

Applying material from Item B and your knowledge, evaluate the usefulness of different Marxist theories in understanding crime and deviance in contemporary society (30 marks; see page 69).

While there is no set way of writing an essay, the following template can be used to answer this type of item-based essay question. It may also be useful for some 20-mark questions on Theory and methods (Question 06). The template is referred to in the commentary on the sample answers in this section.

Template for Paper 3, Questions 04 and 06

Introduction: AAA
- **A:** 'As Item A states…' — In your own words, sum up one or two points from the item.
- **A:** Argument 1 — for the essay above, the Marxist theory of the causes of crime and deviance
- **A:** Argument 2 — for the essay above, the functionalists' view; for example, 'However, functionalists argue that…'

Main body
Paragraphs 1–3 (or more if needed) on Argument 1 — include AO2 and AO3 points in each paragraph.

For each paragraph, develop AO2 and AO3 by using the following techniques:
- Use studies and examples to illustrate strengths and weaknesses of the argument.
- Give **specific** evaluation points on arguments, such as supporting evidence being out of date or that it cannot be generalised easily.
- Give evaluation points from different **sociological perspectives** — how they agree or disagree.
- If applicable, discuss how the argument has been developed internally (for this essay, by different neo–Marxist views on the causes of crime and deviance).

Paragraph 4 (or 5 etc.) on Argument 2 — State how it disagrees/agrees with Argument 1 (for this question, from the functionalist perspective).

Paragraph 5, 6 etc. on other possible arguments — State how they disagree/agree with Argument 1 (for this essay, from the interactionist and right realist perspectives, for example).

Conclusion
- 'Perhaps the **main strength** of Argument 1 is that it is right to point to the importance of…'
- 'Perhaps the **main weakness** of Argument 1, as Argument 2 points out, is that it ignores the impact of…'
- Say **something new**. Try not to just recap previous points in the conclusion. (For this essay, this could be a criticism of the Marxist view of crime and deviance from a feminist perspective, if not previously mentioned.)

The main body of this template is useful for a question that focuses on **evaluating a particular perspective on crime and deviance** (such as different Marxist theories in the question above). You must clearly apply other arguments showing how and the extent to which they agree or disagree with it. If the question requires you to **evaluate sociological explanations** of an issue or to **evaluate a claim**, you should allocate time more equally to the main arguments (see page 54 on question 06).

Depending on the issue raised in the question and the marks available, the number of paragraphs you devote to each argument will vary. As stated, you should not wait until paragraph 4 to use other theories to evaluate; this should be done throughout the essay.

> A good revision strategy is to practise writing essay questions under exam conditions. Allow yourself approximately 45 minutes for question 04. You can use the template to devise your own more detailed plans for essays on other areas outlined in the Content Guidance section.

Question 05

Outline and explain two...

Here is an example:

Outline and explain two reasons why sociology cannot be regarded as a science (10 marks; see page 70).

Remember you only need two paragraphs. No introduction or conclusion is required.

The first paragraph for the question above could be set out as follows:

- First sentence: State what the first reason is. For this question, the first sentence could be as follows: 'The first reason why sociology cannot be a science is that sociology does not have a shared paradigm.'
- AO1: **Explain** — Outline what the first reason is. For example, for this question you could explain the concept of a paradigm and give an example to illustrate.
- AO3: **Analyse** — Unpack this with some discussion of the limitation. For example, for this question you could refer to the work of Kuhn and how different sociological theories and methodological approaches do not have a shared paradigm.
- AO2: **Apply** — Use studies and examples to illustrate this reason. For example, for this question you could use the topic of education to illustrate that Marxists such as Bowles and Gintis will not agree with functionalists on the role of education in transmitting shared values.
- AO3: **Evaluation** — This is *not* required as there are no specific marks for evaluation for this question.

The same structure should be used for paragraph two, which should focus on a separate reason (such as reasons why sociology cannot be a science according to Popper or interpretivists — see page 70).

Expect to find the following types of wording for Question 05.

For a methods question — Outline and explain:

- two advantages/disadvantages of using a specific method (e.g. structured interviews) in sociological research

> Do *not* use words such as 'however' for this question. AO3 marks are only awarded for analysis. However, if evaluation is within an analytical framework it should be credited.

- two advantages/disadvantages of using a specific type of data (e.g. qualitative data) in sociological research
- two ethical/practical/theoretical advantages (or disadvantages) of using a specific method or type of data in sociological research
- two practical/ethical/theoretical problems sociologists may experience when conducting sociological research
- two advantages of choosing one method (e.g. unstructured interviews) as a source of data compared with another method (e.g. structured interviews)

For a theory question — Outline and explain:

- two strengths of a particular theory (e.g. Marxist, functionalist, feminist, interactionist) in understanding contemporary society
- two weaknesses/limitations of a particular theory in understanding contemporary society
- two strengths of a particular type of theory (e.g. conflict, structural, social action) in understanding contemporary society
- two weaknesses/limitations of a particular type of theory in understanding contemporary society

Other questions — Outline and explain:

- two reasons why sociology can/cannot be regarded as a science
- two reasons why sociologists can/cannot be value free in their research
- two ways in which sociological perspectives have influenced social policy

Question 06

Applying material from Item C and your own knowledge, evaluate…

Here is an example:

Applying material from Item C and your own knowledge, evaluate the claim that we are now living in a postmodern society (20 marks; see page 57).

You could use the template for Questions 04 and 06 to construct your own more detailed plan for this type of item-based essay question on sociological theory (see page 51). Remember that the question above requires you to evaluate a **claim** rather than a **specific sociological theory** and the advice given below reflects this.

> You can attempt to write this essay using the template and the advice below under exam conditions. Allow yourself approximately 30 minutes. For a 20-mark question on methods, you could use the WWWE template for your introduction (see Student Guide 1, Education with theory and methods, page 50).

Introduction

As stated in Item C, there have been significant changes in society in the last 50 years or so, such as the increasing influence of the media in shaping our identity [first 'A']. **Postmodernists** argue that as a result, today's society is in fact postmodern [second 'A']. However, **modern theories** such as Marxism argue that we are still in the modern era and, as Item C states, there are features of a modern society such as class, ethnicity and gender that have a major impact on people's life chances in society [third 'A']. Alternatively, **late modernists** argue that while rapid changes have occurred in society, they are not the start of a new, postmodern era — instead, they are actually a continuation of modernity itself [fourth 'A'].

> Note that, rather than having two arguments in the introduction (as in the AAA in the template on page 51), there are three main points of view on this claim of the essay. This introduction therefore requires AAAA (the first 'A' being the reference to the item, followed by the three key arguments on the debate, as indicated).

Main body

Paragraphs 1 and 2. Outline the key aspects of the modern era and modern theories. Use AO2 and AO3 techniques (see template on page 51). **Clearly state how modern theories disagree with the claim of the essay.**

Paragraphs 3 and 4. Outline the postmodern view that we are living in a postmodern society. Use AO2 and AO3 techniques. **Clearly state how this agrees with the claim of the essay.**

Paragraphs 5 and 6. Outline theories of late modernity and how they **agree/disagree with the claim.** Use AO2 and AO3 techniques.

Conclusion

Perhaps the main strength of the postmodernist view that we live in a postmodern society is that it is clear that factors such as globalisation and the increasing significance of the media in shaping our culture and identity do suggest that we are no longer living in a modern era. For example, global social media platforms have become the standard form of communication not only for youth subcultures, but for presidents of powerful nations such as the USA.

Perhaps the main weakness of this argument is identified by the Marxist view that traditional sources of identity of the 'modern era', namely class, still exist and that postmodernists ignore the importance of power and inequality in today's society, such as how the ruling class use the media as a tool of ideological domination.

[Something new] A different view is put forward by postmodern Marxists such as Harvey, who agree with postmodernists that we are now living in a postmodern society. However, rather than seeing postmodernity as a fundamental break with the past, they regard it as the product of the most recent stage of capitalism.

> In your conclusion, do not just recap what you have already written as this will add nothing to your essay. Also, try to avoid using a 'catch-all' point such as 'feminist sociologists would argue that postmodernism is patriarchal'. This is likely to add little as it does not focus on why some feminists would reject the idea of a postmodern society.

Expect to find the following types of wording for Question 06.

For a methods question — Applying material from Item C and your knowledge, evaluate:

- the advantages/disadvantages of using a particular method (e.g. questionnaires) in studying contemporary society
- the advantages/disadvantages of using a particular type of data (e.g. qualitative data) in studying contemporary society
- the advantages/disadvantages of using a particular methodological perspective (i.e. positivist or interpretivist) in studying contemporary society

For a theory question — Applying material from Item C and your knowledge, evaluate:

- the usefulness of a particular theoretical perspective (e.g. Marxist, functionalist, feminist, interactionist approaches) in understanding contemporary society
- the usefulness of a particular type of theoretical approach (e.g. consensus, conflict, structural, social action) in understanding contemporary society
- the view that one particular type of theoretical approach (e.g. conflict approaches) is more useful than other approaches (such as consensus approaches) to our understanding of contemporary society

Other questions — Applying material from Item C and your knowledge, evaluate:

- the claim that sociology can/cannot and should/should not be a science
- the claim that sociology can/cannot and should/should not be value free

■ Test paper 1

(01) Outline **two** reasons why it is difficult to measure state crime. (4 marks)

> Remember to use bullet points and give an extra point if you have time. You could refer to the various ways in which the state has the power to conceal crimes and define its activities as legal (e.g. through 'techniques of neutralisation'). Try to give an example to illustrate each point.

(02) Outline **three** limitations of victim surveys in measuring levels of crime. (6 marks)

> Use bullet points and give an extra point if you have time. Points such as victim surveys lacking validity or representativeness must be explained in terms of how these do not give an accurate picture of crime levels. It may be useful to give examples of the types of crime that victim surveys are not useful for measuring.

(03) Read **Item A** below and answer the question that follows.

Item A

It has been argued that females are controlled in various areas of society, particularly at home and in the workplace. For example, daughters may be more closely controlled in the family and women's career opportunities may be restricted by the 'glass ceiling'. However, it has been argued that as society is becoming less patriarchal, women are adopting more traditionally male attitudes and behaviours.

Applying material from **Item A**, analyse **two** reasons that may influence whether females commit crime.

(10 marks)

You should spend about 15 minutes on this question. Divide your time fairly equally between each reason and write a paragraph on each. You could structure each paragraph as suggested on page 50. There is no need to write a separate introduction or conclusion. You are only required to give two reasons, and these must be applied from material in the item.

The first 'hook' in Item A is the reference to females being 'controlled in various areas of society'. This should lead to a discussion of the work of Heidensohn or Carlen — for example, how working-class women may be controlled by the gender and class 'deals'. This *must* be applied to how this may influence females to commit crime — for example, how the gender and class deals do apply to most women and therefore they don't make the choice to commit crime (a choice which would be rational if they lacked those deals). This could be evaluated by reference to criticisms from sex role theory or by pointing out that this approach portrays women as passive victims of social control.

The second 'hook' in Item A is the reference to society 'becoming less patriarchal' and women 'adopting more traditionally male attitudes and behaviours'. This should lead to a discussion of Adler's liberation theory — for example, that as society is becoming less patriarchal, women have more equal opportunities in society. This *must* be applied to how this may influence whether females commit crime — for example, that as women are gaining greater equality in the labour market and engaging in risk-taking behaviour, they may be more likely to commit crimes. This could be evaluated by reference to the argument of some feminists that increased marginalisation rather than liberation is the reason why females are committing more crime.

(04) Read **Item B** below and answer the question that follows.

Item B

Realist approaches view crime as a real and growing problem and not just a social construction. Right realists argue that due to factors such as the inadequate socialisation of some people, crime, particularly in urban areas, is a serious problem that needs addressing.

However, left realists, while agreeing that governments need to be tough on crime, argue that social policies should also be tough on the causes of crime.

Applying material from **Item B** and your knowledge, evaluate the usefulness of realist approaches to crime and crime prevention.

(30 marks)

You should spend about 45 minutes on this question. It may be helpful to use the template for an item-based essay question on page 51. Use the item to introduce the similarities and differences between right and left realists. You should outline and compare the different arguments each has on both the causes of crime and the solutions to crime. As well as criticisms from other perspectives, such as Marxist, interactionist and feminist perspectives, you should also give specific evaluation points on the arguments of both types of realist. Rather than simply listing other theories or explanations of crime and deviance, you should discuss how they have differing views on both the causes of crime and the solutions to crime.

(05) Outline and explain **two** limitations of Marxist approaches to our understanding of contemporary society. (10 marks)

You should spend about 15 minutes on this question. Divide your time fairly equally between each limitation and write a paragraph on each. You could structure each paragraph as suggested on page 52. You should only write about two limitations. There is no need to write a separate introduction or conclusion.

As well as specific limitations, such as some Marxist approaches being economically deterministic, you could refer to criticisms from other perspectives, such as the feminist view that they ignore gender inequality. As the question wording refers to 'approaches', you could discuss neo-Marxist critiques of the traditional Marxist view.

Topics studied, such as education, could be used to illustrate the limitations of the Marxist view. For example, Althusser's argument that the education system is an ideological state apparatus which is used to legitimate inequalities in capitalist society could be analysed through a comparison with the functionalist view of the positive aspects of the socialisation function of education (using Durkheim or Parsons). Remember that no marks are awarded for evaluation for this question.

(06) Read **Item C** and answer the question that follows.

Item C

Postmodernists argue that due to the significant changes that have taken place in society, the modern era has come to an end. This, it is claimed, is due to factors such as the rapid social and economic changes that took place in the later part of the twentieth century. For example, there has been a shift to a post-Fordist economy and a media-saturated society.

However, other sociologists acknowledge that while rapid changes have occurred since the 1970s, factors such as social class inequalities are still significant in contemporary society.

Applying material from **Item C** and your own knowledge, evaluate the claim that we are now living in a postmodern society. (20 marks)

You should spend about 30 minutes on this question. It may be helpful to use the template on page 51: see also pages 53–54 for further guidance. A good place to start would be to outline the characteristics of the 'modern era' using the item and explain how these have changed with the impact of globalisation. Make sure that, as well as evaluation from other theories such as Marxism, functionalism, late modernism, and postmodern Marxism, you include specific evaluation of the postmodern view. Material relating to other perspectives *must* be applied to how they agree or disagree with the postmodern view that we are living in a postmodern society.

The impact of the media is obviously a key topic area to use to discuss the debate regarding whether we are in a modern, late-modern or postmodern society, but you should also apply other topic areas studied such as education and crime and deviance. For example, you could discuss how the education system is arguably more diverse now and has moved away from the 'one size fits all approach' of the comprehensive system that existed at the end of the 'modern era' in the 1970s.

Student answer

(01) ■ In the name of national security or the public interest, governments have the power to cover up their crimes so they can't be measured. For example, they may put pressure on the media or put legal restrictions on journalists reporting on activities such as detaining terrorists illegally without trial.

■ The government may appeal to higher loyalties. For example, Israeli or Islamic-led governments might argue that they have a divine right to commit acts of war on civilians to defend their 'God-given' territory. Therefore, these crimes may not be seen as illegal by their citizens.

> Two appropriate points explained with examples.
> **4/4 marks awarded**

(02) ■ They do not include victimless crimes. People who have been robbed in the course of their drug habit or prostitution are unlikely to state that they have been involved in these activities.

■ Marxists argue that they will lack validity as people are often not aware that they have been the victim of corporate crimes or crimes by the state so will not mention them in the survey.

■ It does not include victims of commercial crime and so is not a representative picture of all criminal activity. For example, it does not include crimes such as theft from shops.

> Three appropriate points are explained with examples.
> **6/6 marks awarded**

(03) As stated in Item A, females may be 'controlled in various areas of society'. For feminists such as Heidensohn, patriarchal control within the home is a major reason why females commit less crimes than males. Perhaps the biggest control on females is that the housewife/mother role is still considered to be the primary role for females. Heidensohn argues that as a result of women being confined to the home, they have little time to engage in criminal activities. The cycle continues for young girls as they are subject to double standards such as earlier curfew times than for male siblings and so again, they are less likely to be 'on the street' where there are greater opportunities to commit crime. As the study by Dobash and Dobash shows, males are able to exercise their power over women through domestic violence which they are often unable to escape due to the financial control their male partner has. Again this ties women to the home and means they will be the victim rather than the perpetrator of crimes. However, this view can be considered as outdated as there has been an increase in the number of career women and househusbands. Also, the lives of teenage girls are less likely to revolve around a bedroom culture today as illustrated by the increase in girl gangs.

Another feminist, Carlen, argues that women have access to gender or class deals. As a result of the class deal, some working-class women were likely to make the rational choice to commit crime as they didn't have the financial security that a middle-class housewife would have. If they had no qualifications or career opportunities, they could not be financially independent. Women who don't have access to the class deal may therefore commit crime. A criticism of Carlen is that she does not explain why some women in poverty don't commit crime.

There is good coverage of two differing types of control that feminists identify which have been explained and evaluated. However, while the first is clearly linked to the hook in the item, the second point on Carlen is not. It is possible to make two separate points from the same hook in the item (and therefore score above 7 marks) but the point on Carlen does not make a reference to Item A. This demonstrates that it is a good strategy to directly quote the hooks from the item for this question.

7/10 marks awarded

(04) As Item B states, both right and left realists see crime as a serious problem and argue that theories such as labelling theory, that see crime as a social construction, are too sympathetic to criminals. Rather than seeing the police as part of the problem, realists argue that they have a key role in preventing neighbourhood decline and in bringing about crime reduction. However, while right realists (RRs) feel this can be achieved through zero tolerance policing and environmental crime prevention strategies such as repairing 'broken windows', left realists (LRs) prefer social and community crime prevention strategies such as using police community support officers (PCSOs). Another key difference is that while RRs believe that crime can only be controlled, LRs argue that social policies can help reduce crime by removing the conditions which predispose people to commit crime, such as being socially excluded due to lack of educational opportunities. In this respect, LRs agree with Marxists that social inequalities need to be addressed. However, Marxists reject both left and right realism for ignoring corporate crime.

This is a very good, evaluative introduction which follows the item-based essay template on page 51. The item is applied in relation to both aspects of the question, the realist approaches to the causes of crime and crime prevention.

RRs like Wilson and Herrnstein argue that biological differences make some people more likely to deviate and commit crime. RRs argue that it is a personality trait. Aggressive people are more likely therefore to commit violent crimes such as assault. Furthermore, RRs claim that people with low intelligence don't understand the significance of rewards and punishments. This makes it more likely they will deviate. However, Lilly found that only 3% of differences in offending could be explained by differences in intelligence levels. This calls into question the usefulness of the view that intelligence is biologically determined and can cause crime. RRs agree with functionalists and New Right theorists that not everyone is effectively socialised, so some people are prone to deviate. Effective socialisation through nuclear families decreases the risk of offending as it teaches the correct values. However, New Right theorist Murray argues that the nuclear family is undermined by the welfare state which creates a dependent underclass who are more likely to commit crime. Generous welfare provision increases the number of lone-parent families, and absent fathers means boys lack a role model. Subcultural theorists argue that they may turn to deviant groups and commit crime as a result.

While labelling theorists argue that labelling someone as deviant encourages them to commit crime, RRs like Clarke argue that we have free will and committing crime is a rational choice. If the rewards outweigh the costs (if punishments are too lenient) then people will choose to offend. Furthermore, Felton's routine activity theory states that a crime only occurs if there is a motivated offender, a suitable target and the absence of a capable guardian such as a police officer. This supports the idea that crime requires a calculated way of thinking and the offender must be committed to the act. However, the RR theory contradicts itself — criminals can't have rational choice if their behaviour is determined by biological factors and poor socialisation.

Like Marxists, LRs such as Lea and Young argue that RRs ignore the wider structural causes of crime such as poverty and social exclusion. LRs argue that a major cause of crime is relative deprivation, where people feel resentment because other people have got what they haven't. The media make us aware of the latest consumer goods that some socially deprived groups cannot afford. In addition, LRs argue that deprived groups, particularly minority ethnic groups, may turn to crime due to feeling marginalised as a result of being socially excluded. This may lead to the formation of what LRs identify as the third cause of crime: subcultures. For example, young, black, unemployed males may experience relative deprivation and marginalisation as a result of what they feel is a racist society. Due to their unemployment (caused by what they feel are racist teachers and employers), they cannot afford the 'bling' that they see others have. As a result of being 'on the street', they may seek a collective response and form deviant subcultures and use illegitimate opportunity structures to achieve success based on street crime. However, a criticism of the LR view on the causes of crime is that it does not explain why some working-class people who are relatively deprived commit crime and others do not. Marxists are critical of LRs for borrowing ideas from functionalists and subcultural theory, such as blocked opportunities to mainstream values, and argue that they have abandoned any links with Marxism and are not really 'left wing' at all.

A good coverage of two RR causes of crime: biological factors and socialisation. However, while there is some brief analysis, such as the comparison with other perspectives, there is only one specific evaluation point (on intelligence).

The third RR cause of crime is reasonably presented but there is limited analysis. This could have been related to control theory and crime prevention.

A sound explanation of the LR view on the causes of crime with some good analysis and evaluation.

RRs such as Wilson and Kelling argue that environmental crime prevention (ECP) is the best way to reduce crime. They claim that leaving broken windows unrepaired sends a signal that no one cares, which encourages further crime. An environmental improvement strategy helps to solve this by dealing with disorder immediately. For example, broken windows need repairing straight away. This was evident in New York through the 'clean car program', in which subway carriages were taken out of service if they had graffiti on them, which led to a reduction of graffiti. ECP also involves a 'zero tolerance' policy, which means the police must tackle the slightest signs of disorder to prevent more serious crimes. Although 'zero tolerance' policing caused some crimes to drop by 60% in New York, not all crimes reduced. Furthermore, the reduction of crime may have been a result of bringing in 7,000 new police officers rather than the policy itself. While LRs agree with RRs that the police can help reduce neighbourhood decline and people's fear of crime, they would argue that the RR zero tolerance policy allows the police to discriminate against particular groups like minority ethnic groups and can damage community relations. LRs would also argue that this strategy ignores the causes of crime such as poverty.

> A good coverage of ECP which is evaluated and explained with appropriate examples. A good comparison between RR and LR approaches but this could have been done more often.

In addition, RRs like Clarke also encourage the use of situational crime prevention (SCP) to reduce crime. This is a strategy for reducing opportunities for crime by managing the immediate environment to increase the risks for criminals and reduce the rewards. However, this assumes criminals commit crime based on rational choice, which may not be the case if the criminal was under the influence of drugs. This strategy also involves 'target hardening' as a measure to deter criminals from committing crime. For example, using CCTV in shops makes it more likely shoplifters will be caught which may deter them. However, the concept of 'displacement' shows that this strategy is not very useful as criminals may simply move to places where targets are softer. For example, Chaiken et al. argue that a crackdown on subway robberies in New York simply displaced criminals to the streets above. However, in Stoke an SCP strategy of increasing street lighting did not result in displacement. The crime rate went down by 26% in the area with increased lighting but also fell in the surrounding area by over 20%, suggesting that displacement does not always occur. Marxists however would criticise situational crime prevention policies for enabling the middle classes to 'design' crime out of their lives. By having gated communities, a new type of social inequality is created where those who can afford it are 'safe' whereas working-class people continue to be the main victims of crime.

> Again, good analysis of an RR crime prevention strategy. There are several very good attempts to evaluate, mainly on specific aspects of the policy but also from a Marxist perspective.

On the other hand, LRs prefer social and community crime prevention strategies (SCCPs) as a way of reducing crime. These often involve a long-term strategy with an aim to tackle the root causes of offending, such as poverty, rather than simply removing opportunities for crime as in the RR strategy. Furthermore, they aim to tackle social exclusion and reduce the 'fear of crime' through strategies such as curfew times in ASBOs and the use of PCSOs. However, a criticism of PCSOs is that they are not always taken seriously in comparison to police officers. An example of social and community crime prevention in practice is the Perry Preschool project. This involved disadvantaged black children in the USA having an intellectual enrichment programme and home visits. As a result, these children had fewer arrests and better employment over their lifetime than peers who didn't follow the programme. In the UK, 'third way' New Labour policies such as Sure Start were heavily influenced by the ideas of LR. The aim was to give marginalised people in society a 'hand up not a handout' by providing nursery care so single parents could work but also to give better educational opportunities. The aim of Sure Start along with Aim Higher and EMA was to try to provide the socially excluded with better educational opportunities so that they could avoid turning to crime in later life. Also, if people feel that society is fair they are less likely to suffer from relative deprivation and feel marginalised and so are less likely to commit crime. However, Marxists claim that social and community crime prevention measures such as community policing focus too much on petty street crime and ignore corporate crime. RRs would reject LR as being too soft on criminals and would argue that crime is an individual's choice due to poor values and is not caused by inequalities in society. As has been outlined, they would favour policies that are tougher on crime, such as harsher punishments and increased control. While LRs call for tackling discrimination by providing jobs to reduce crime and deviance, RRs believe it is pointless to tackle underlying causes. Another problem with policies such as the Perry Preschool project is that it takes a long time to see the results in terms of crime prevention. Perhaps the main strength of RR is that criminals do use 'rational choice' when committing crimes and that SCP strategies of 'target hardening' such as CCTV and locking doors will make it much more difficult for burglars to commit crimes. However, perhaps the main weakness of RRs, as LRs argue, is that they fail to take account of inequalities that cause crime and deviance to occur and that policies to tackle social exclusion such as Sure

> Some good application of examples of LR policies that have been well evaluated from different perspectives.

Start will help reduce crime, if only in the longer term. However, RRs would argue that the LR idea of social and community crime prevention is not tough enough on crime. For example, PCSOs are not feared enough to deter criminals from committing crime. Feminists would reject realist theories, arguing they ignore female crime and crime prevention. They would be particularly critical of the RR focus on the effect of absent fathers on their sons and would argue that most realist crime prevention strategies are 'malestream' as they tend to focus on reducing male crime. Dobash and Dobash's study on domestic violence revealed how this crime was hidden and largely ignored by society and social policy.

A good conclusion which is evaluative and identifies some key strengths and weaknesses of realist approaches to both causes of crime and solutions to crime. The point could have been made that LRs are less 'malestream' than RRs as they acknowledge that relative deprivation, marginalisation and subculture can lead to crimes that affect females such as domestic violence.

Overall a detailed coverage of RR and LR ideas on the causes of crime and solutions to crime, which overall have been well evaluated with specific examples and by using other perspectives. The issues of crime being a real problem and the fear of crime could have been covered in more depth, as well as the realist argument that official statistics reflect real rates of crime. At times the realist views are presented by juxtaposition. A better strategy would have been to compare their views on issues in each paragraph, which would have developed a stronger comparison of the two realist approaches on the question set. However, there is enough analysis and evaluation to score 30 marks.

30/30 marks awarded

(05) One limitation of the Marxist approach to our understanding of society is that they are wrong to believe that society is based on conflict. Marxists believe that society is unfair and that the bourgeoisie exploit the proletariat in the workplace. They would argue that the function of the education system is to legitimate and reproduce class inequalities. For example, Bowles and Gintis argued that there is a myth of meritocracy and that the working class underachieve. Functionalists such as Davis and Moore would reject this conflict view and argue that education is meritocratic (e.g. the examination system offers equal opportunities) and individuals are 'sifted and sorted' into their appropriate role in the workplace. As well as the selection function, Parsons points to the socialisation function of education and how this can be positive in terms of socialising individuals into universalistic values and so acting as a bridge between the family and society. Rather than transmitting ruling-class ideology as Althusser suggests, functionalists argue that the education system passes on shared values. Therefore, the education system has positive functions for society rather than negative. A limitation of the Marxist approach for functionalists is that contemporary society is based on consensus and shared values rather than being based on conflict.

A second limitation is that the theory is too 'macro' and only focuses on structural factors, so cannot be used to explain behaviour at an individual level. Marxism is based on examining the effects of the wider social structure, such as how capitalism is criminogenic and will inevitably lead to the working class committing crime, and how the education system leads to the reproduction of class inequality and the myth of meritocracy. Interactionists would argue that Marxism fails to look at micro factors such as teacher labelling and the impact this has on working-class students underachieving. This therefore means that Marxism cannot be used to understand how contemporary society functions, as it is restricted to looking at how structural processes, rather than individual actions, can be used to explain social problems.

The student has a good knowledge and understanding of two limitations of Marxism. Both paragraphs are structured well, with a brief account of the Marxist view and then a criticism of this from another perspective. There is appropriate analysis and application of these through the topic of education. A good strategy is to apply more than one topic area to the limitation. For example, the reference to crime in paragraph two could have been developed and compared with the interactionist view on the causes of crime. More detail was needed in the second paragraph to achieve the maximum mark. The criticism from interactionists could have been developed with a more in-depth discussion of teacher labelling.
9/10 marks awarded

(06) As stated in Item C, postmodernists argue that today's society is in fact postmodern: a globalised, media-saturated society in which signs become hyperreal with no reference to society. However, modern theories such as Marxism argue that we are still in the modern era and, as Item C states, there are features of a modern society such as class, ethnicity and gender that have a major impact on people's life chances in society.

A good, evaluative introduction. See page 54 for an introduction that also includes the late-modern view on this question.

The so-called modern era developed after the period of industrialisation which was based on the capitalist mode of production. This revolved around manufacturing and developments in science and rational thought that are referred to as the Enlightenment project. This is the idea that rational thought through scientific positivist methodology could lead to progress in society. This is illustrated in the work of early positivist sociologists such as Marx and Durkheim who were part of the modern era. Marx argued that capitalism was a key aspect of modern society. Capitalism brought about the industrialisation of modern society. However, postmodernists argue that the economy has changed from Fordist (with assembly lines) to post-Fordist, with a more diverse workforce being required rather than the unskilled labour force required by capitalism in the modern era. They would argue that in a postmodern society there has been a decline in traditional manufacturing and that the education system has responded to the needs of a diverse, global economy by offering different types of schools, such as technology colleges, and more apprenticeships.

A fair discussion of characteristics of the modern era with some evaluation from a postmodern perspective.

Another key aspect of the modern era is the idea of the nation-state being a focal point of modern society, organising social life on a national basis. Postmodernists, however, argue that globalisation has also undermined the power of the nation-state, as it is now less able to regulate the activities of large capitalist enterprises such as transnational companies. Postmodernists also argue that globalisation has led to a change from a modern to a postmodern society in other ways. As well as changes in the global economy, globalisation has also led to changes in culture and identity through the increased influence of the media. Baudrillard argues that society is now based on buying and selling knowledge in the form of images and signs promoted via the media. These images and signs, however, bear no relation to physical reality in today's society. This is described as hyperreality, which involves our inability to distinguish between image and reality. However, postmodernists argue it is wrong to say people can't distinguish between reality and media images. In a postmodern society, identity has also become destabilised as we can easily change it through the 'pick and mix' culture that our media-saturated world offers us. However, Marxists would argue that this overlooks the impact of social class and that poverty can restrict opportunities and access to cultural goods.

> A good discussion of how globalisation has impacted on modern society. However, the section on postmodernism and identity could have been developed.

Theories of late modernity reject the essay claim and argue that key features of modernity still exist but have now intensified. Giddens believes that in the late-modern era, a process of disembedding has occurred. We no longer need face-to-face contact in order to interact as this can be achieved through things such as the new media, for example social networking sites and online shopping. As traditions that were prominent in the 19th and 20th centuries and class culture are no longer an important influence on our lives, we are forced to become reflexive. This means that we have to constantly monitor, reflect on and modify our actions in the light of information. This happens in the workplace through things such as performance management and also in self-assessment activities that students do to improve their grades in school. However, Marxists would argue that not everyone has the option to be reflexive and that social class is still the key influence on whether we are able to have such choices in our lifestyles. Access to the new media is dependent on social class, as those who are exploited by the capitalist system, such as those on zero-hour contracts, will not be able to afford the latest iPhone or Sky broadband package. This is an example of how Marxists would argue that we are still in the modern era rather than living in a late-modern or postmodern society.

> The late-modern view is applied to the question and there are some good evaluation points from a Marxist perspective.

Another late-modern theorist, Beck, believes we now live in a risk society. As well as helping to keep people close together, globalisation also brings risks such as greenhouse gases which contribute to global climate change. Beck argues we are now increasingly endangered from human-made technology rather than natural disasters, which recognises negative impacts of globalisation. There are manufactured risks from human activity, such as global warming. As a result, we have to think for ourselves and become aware, for instance by reading about the benefits of living an environmentally friendly lifestyle and looking at information on how to lower the risks to our lives (e.g. by healthy eating). Much of this knowledge, however, comes from the media, which Marxists argue can give a distorted, pro-capitalist view. Like Giddens, Beck believes we are capable of reflexivity — we can take political action to bring about change such as getting involved in environmental groups and other forms of protest. Late-modern theories reject the postmodern view of society, and the claim of the essay, as they argue that rational analysis of society remains possible and we can use knowledge to improve society and reduce the risks we face. However, Hirst says we are unable to bring about any significant change because we are too fragmented to challenge capitalism.

Marxists would argue that this notion is just another example of how ruling-class ideology brainwashes us into believing that we can bring about change in capitalist society. They would argue that signing a petition on Change.org is not going to have any real impact on inequality in capitalism and this illustrates that we are not living in a postmodern society.

> The late-modern view is developed further with some comparison with the postmodern and Marxist views. There is some good application to the question.

However, some Marxists take a different view of the changes that have taken place in society and agree with late-modern and postmodern ideas in that they accept that capitalist society has changed from how it was in the modern era. Marxist theories of postmodernity have similar views to Beck and Giddens, in that capitalism has changed and has 'new risks'. However, like postmodernists they believe that capitalism has moved from modernity to postmodernity. However, rather than seeing postmodernity as a fundamental break with the past, they regard it as the product of the most recent stage of capitalism. Postmodern Marxists see flexible accumulation as a new way of achieving profitability which has replaced the Fordist system based on mass production such as the assembly lines of the car industry. This involves the increased use of ICT, job insecurity and workers needing to be flexible to fit their employers' needs. This is illustrated through the idea of zero-hour contracts, which they would regard as a postmodern form of exploitation. This has brought changes in consumption, for example of fashion, music and sports, which are now an important source of profit. However, Harvey argues that this is a more developed form of capitalism which also leads to another feature of postmodernity, time–space compression. Postmodern Marxists therefore agree with postmodernists that we are now living in a postmodern society. However, they argue that recent changes in society can be explained by how the nature of capitalism has changed and adapted to postmodern society. They reject the postmodernist view of how popular culture is used in a positive way to shape our identities. Rather, postmodern Marxists and traditional Marxists would argue that conspicuous consumption is the result of mass culture being forced onto us by the media. This results in commodity fetishism where, rather than meeting our needs, the media create needs for the benefit of capitalism. For example, the 'need' for us to buy the latest iPhone will create more profit for capitalists.

> This is a good and detailed discussion of the view of Marxist postmodernists which is well applied to the question. Other aspects of flexible accumulation, such as how it also brought about political changes (e.g. weakened working-class and socialist movements), could have been mentioned.

Perhaps the main strength of the postmodernist view that we live in a postmodern society is that it is clear that factors such as globalisation and the increasing significance of the media in shaping our culture and identity do suggest that we are no longer living in a modern era. For example, the new media have significantly changed areas of our lives such as how we communicate, shop and learn. However, Marxists would argue that traditional sources of identity, namely class, still exist and that postmodernists ignore the importance of power and inequality in today's society, such as how the ruling class use the media as a tool of domination. Postmodern Marxist theories build on the postmodernist view by relating the recent changes in society to the nature of capitalism. However, it could be argued that they abandon Marx's original view of the Enlightenment project and a dictatorship by the proletariat. Therefore, the question could be asked, are they really Marxist if they accept that we are now living in a postmodern stage of capitalism?

> This is a good conclusion which attempts to give examples to back up the student's view of the main strengths and weaknesses of postmodern and Marxist views on the question. However, late-modern and other perspectives could have been mentioned.

Overall there is some good coverage of postmodern, Marxist, late-modern and postmodern Marxist views which have been applied to the question. However, there could have been more focus on the postmodern view and the student has not mentioned other sociological perspectives that were part of the modern era, such as functionalist and feminist views. As well as continued gender inequality, other aspects of the modern era could also have been discussed, such as the significance of ethnicity. The issue of modern theories being metanarratives offering no 'truth' as far as postmodernists are concerned has only been briefly referred to. See page 54 for more guidance on how to structure this essay. Despite these limitations, there is enough analysis and evaluation for maximum marks.
20/20 marks awarded

Total score: 76/80. This response is likely to be awarded an A* grade.

■Test paper 2

(01) Outline **two** ways that globalisation may lead to an increase in crime. (4 marks)

> Remember to use bullet points and give an extra point if you have time. You could refer to an increase in crimes resulting from issues such as deregulation, outsourcing, international terrorism and trafficking, and also note how globalisation has created new offences such as cybercrimes. Try to give an example and ensure you refer to global factors increasing crime.

(02) Outline **three** functions that punishment may perform for society. (6 marks)

> Remember to use bullet points and give an extra point if you have time. As well as functions such as deterrence, incapacitation and rehabilitation, you could refer to how Marxists view punishments as serving the needs of capitalism. Try to give an example of a punishment to illustrate the function that it performs for society.

(03) Read **Item A** below and answer the question that follows.

Item A

> The role of the criminal justice system is to identify, catch and punish unlawful individuals. It consists of institutions such as the police, courts and prison. Conviction rates for different social groups may be influenced by factors such as social exclusion and inequalities in society.

Applying material from **Item A**, analyse **two** reasons for ethnic differences in criminal conviction rates. (10 marks)

> You should spend about 15 minutes on this question. Divide your time fairly equally between the two reasons and write a paragraph on each. You could structure each paragraph as suggested on page 50. There is no need to write a separate introduction or conclusion. You are only required to give two reasons, and these must be applied from material in the item.
>
> The first 'hook' in Item A is the reference to the 'criminal justice system' (CJS). This should lead to a discussion of how the CJS can discriminate against minority ethnic groups (MEGs), which may lead to them appearing disproportionally in the official crime statistics. For example, you could discuss how the police may believe the 'myth of black criminality' (Gilroy) and so be more likely to stop and search people in the black community, or how the 'moral panic' regarding black muggers (Hall) was brought about by the activities of the police and media labelling. This *must* be applied to how this may have led to ethnic differences in criminal conviction rates — for example, by showing how these two processes would have increased conviction rates for people in the black community. This could be evaluated by reference to right and left realist arguments that these neo-Marxist views are too sympathetic to the criminal and that black crime is not politically motivated.

The second 'hook' in Item A is the reference to 'social exclusion and inequalities in society'. This should lead to a discussion of the left realist view that while statistics on ethnic differences in conviction rates are accurate, they also may reflect how racism in society has led to certain MEGs being socially excluded. For example, you could note that certain MEGs may face racism in society that leads to marginalisation and relative deprivation. This *must* be applied to how this may have led to ethnic differences in criminal conviction rates. For example, you could discuss how higher levels of unemployment and poverty may lead to real differences in relative deprivation which can lead to higher levels of offending. This could be evaluated by reference to the neo-Marxist view that left realists underestimate the impact of police racism, or criticisms from a right realist perspective.

(04) Read **Item B** below and answer the question that follows.

Item B

For traditional Marxists the very nature of capitalist society causes crime and deviance. The ruling class not only have the power to exploit the working class but are able to make and enforce laws in their own interests.

However, neo-Marxist theories generally take a less deterministic approach and some call for a 'fully social' theory of deviance.

Applying material from **Item B** and your knowledge, evaluate the usefulness of different Marxist theories in understanding crime and deviance in contemporary society. (30 marks)

You should spend about 45 minutes on this question. It may be helpful to use the template for an item-based essay question on page 51. Use the first two sentences of the item to introduce the traditional Marxist view, but don't simply copy the material. As well as outlining how capitalism is criminogenic and uses selective law making and enforcement as stated in the item, you should also refer to the ideological functions of crime and the law. Use the last line of the item to introduce the neo-Marxist views of Taylor, Walton and Young. This can be developed through a discussion of the attempts to apply the fully social theory by Hall and Gilroy in their neo-Marxist studies of ethnicity and crime.

You should refer to the criticisms of different Marxist views from other perspectives, including left and right realists. Rather than simply listing the explanations of crime and deviance offered by other perspectives, you should discuss how they have different views on the causes of crime and deviance. Also, discuss the similarities between theories, such as between interactionist theory and Marxism and their emphasis on the law being selectively enforced by powerful agents of social control.

(05) Outline and explain **two** reasons why sociology cannot be regarded as a science. (10 marks)

> You should spend about 15 minutes on this question. Divide your time fairly equally between the two reasons and write a paragraph on each. You could structure each paragraph as suggested on page 52. You should only write about two reasons and there is no need to write a separate introduction or conclusion.
>
> A good way to structure your answer is to base one paragraph on interpretivist criticisms of the positivist view that sociology can be an objective science, and the second paragraph on alternative views on the nature of science, such as Popper or Kuhn or the postmodernist view. For the interpretivist paragraph, you could use the case study of suicide and refer to arguments from interactionists and ethnomethodologists as to why this topic cannot be studied in a scientific way. Alternatively, you could write one paragraph on Popper and one paragraph on Kuhn. Remember there are no marks for evaluation for this question.

(06) Read **Item C** and answer the question that follows.

> **Item C**
>
> Interactionists argue that rather than being controlled like puppets, individuals have free will, and that society is constructed through people's interactions. They tend to adopt a micro approach to understanding society and use qualitative methods to uncover the meanings people give to their actions.
>
> However, other sociologists advocate taking a 'top-down' approach and reject these methods as being unscientific and unreliable.

Applying material from **Item C** and your knowledge, evaluate the usefulness of interactionist theories and research for our understanding of contemporary society. (20 marks)

> You should spend about 30 minutes on this question. It may be helpful to use the template for an item-based essay question on page 51. A good way to start would be to outline the basic arguments of symbolic interactionists such as Mead and Blumer. This could then be developed via application of topic areas such as education and crime and deviance — for example, how Becker argues that 'underdogs' in society are labelled by agencies of social control such as teachers and police. This could be evaluated by reference to other theoretical views on issues such as the causes of working-class underachievement and patterns of crime, for instance Marxist and functionalist views.
>
> Other versions of social action theory, such as Goffman, phenomenology and ethnomethodology, could then be compared with symbolic interactionism and evaluated. Ensure that you include a section on the research methods used by interactionists. Again, topic areas such as education and crime and deviance could be used to discuss the interpretivist versus positivist methodological debate.

Student answer

(01) ■ Globalisation can lead to an increase in crime as in a postmodern era, countries are more connected through developments in transport and media. For example, the drugs trade has increased as drugs can be transported more easily around the world, increasing opportunities to commit this type of crime. Similarly, drugs can be purchased online on the 'dark web'.

■ Globalisation has meant that it is easier for TNCs to outsource, i.e. relocate their factories to developing countries. This can lead to an increase in crime as not only can TNCs more easily break health and safety laws and exploit workers in these countries (paying less than the legal minimum wage) but it may encourage insecure workers to turn to crime due to their increased poverty.

Two points are explained with examples. There is actually too much detail here as two examples have been given for each point.
4/4 marks awarded

(02) ■ Deterrence. The fact that harsh punishments, such as long prison sentences, may stop reoffending may be functional for society because crime will be reduced as criminals are made an example of.

■ Incapacitation. If someone is put in prison or (more controversially) is chemically castrated, it has the function of making people feel safer in society as they know that that individual is no longer able to offend again.

■ Rehabilitation. If the punishment is used to reform offenders (e.g. through education or therapy), it can have the function of enabling them to make a positive contribution to society through working rather than going back to a life of crime.

Three appropriate points, with examples, have been made.
6/6 marks awarded

(03) The first reason for ethnic differences in criminal conviction rates is, as Item A states, the 'criminal justice system' (CJS). Research suggests that some minority ethnic groups (MEGs) may be treated more severely by the CJS and that this is the reason why they are more likely to appear in the crime statistics. Neo-Marxists such as Gilroy argue that black criminality is a myth created by racist stereotypes held by the police. Those in the CJS, such as the police and courts, act on these stereotypes resulting in MEGs being criminalised, which is reflected in the crime statistics. For example, research suggests that black people are seven times more likely than white people to be stopped and searched by the police. As a result, they are more likely to be charged and convicted of an offence. Similarly, Holdaway observed a racist 'canteen culture' in the police which led to black people being over-policed. This is supported by the fact that the Metropolitan Police admitted that they were institutionally racist after the Macpherson inquiry in to the Stephen Lawrence case. This type of policing has arguably been applied to the Asian community too. For example, in 2004, stop and searches of Asian people rose by over 300% under terrorism laws. This could be due to the police being influenced by the moral panic of Islamophobia. Hall's research on the moral panic about black muggers also shows how media stereotyping may have influenced the police and led to the higher conviction rates of black males in the 1970s. However, right realists would argue that neo-Marxists like Gilroy are too sympathetic to black criminals and that the CJS cannot be blamed for their higher offending rates. They argue that this is due to factors such as them being more likely to be part of an underclass. Left realists would also reject this view and would argue that criminal conviction rates of MEGs are not socially constructed by the police but reflect real levels of offending due to social exclusion.

The second reason for ethnic differences in criminal conviction rates is the impact of society. As Item A states, crime rates may be influenced by 'social exclusion and inequalities in society'. Left realists would argue that crime rates reflect real patterns in offending but that the reason why MEGs commit more crime is that they are socially excluded due to racism in society. For example, a young, unemployed, black male may feel marginalised due to not being able to get a job (because of racist employers) and having no one to represent their interests. Their lack of money, due to being unemployed, may lead to relative deprivation as they are not able to afford the consumer goods that they see advertised in the media. This can lead to higher levels of offending due to their powerlessness and poverty. Their offending may increase if they end up in a deviant subculture, which left realists Lea and Young argued was the third cause of crime. For example, they might join up with other young black males who are also unemployed and have the same feelings of being marginalised. Similarly, it could be argued that Islamophobia has increased the levels of marginalisation experienced by some sections of the Asian community, which may have led to them committing crime. Therefore, as a result of being socially excluded, conviction rates for MEGs may be higher. However, neo-Marxists such as Gilroy argue that left realists underestimate the impact of institutional racism in the police and that the CJS is the real cause of the higher offending rates of MEGs. Right realists, on the other hand, would argue that the cause of higher levels of offending for some MEGs is more due to poor socialisation, rather than to being socially excluded.

Both reasons are well explained and follow the structure suggested on page 50. There is good analysis of the reasons as well as application from the item. The response identifies reasons for differences for conviction rates for two different MEGs and has two good evaluation points for each reason.
10/10 marks awarded

(04) As stated in Item B, traditional Marxists (TMs) argue that capitalism causes crime. They believe that the bourgeoisie are able to make laws for their own benefit, such as being able to exploit workers, and that this is not only criminal but will inevitably cause crime. However, as the item suggests, neo-Marxists (NMs) don't fully support the TM view and argue that sociologists should adopt a fully social theory by using interactionist approaches to studying the causes of crime and deviance. On the other hand, theories such as functionalism and right realism reject Marxist theories' emphasis on capitalism being the cause of crime and argue that factors such as poor socialisation are to blame.

> This is a good introduction that follows the template suggested on page 51. It sets up the debates not only between Marxist theories but with other sociological explanations.

TMs believe that capitalism is criminogenic — by its very nature it causes crime. The bourgeoisie's main aim is to maximise profit (surplus value) so they will exploit workers which will result in workers being in poverty. Gordon argues that crime is the rational response to this inequality. In addition, as the Frankfurt School argue, the media promote false needs which means the working class feel pressured to purchase the latest consumer goods that they may not be able to afford. This explanation is useful as it illustrates how capitalism can cause crime due to its emphasis on competition and materialism. It also explains how capitalism causes crime among all social class groups. For example, white-collar crimes such as tax evasion and corporate crimes such as price fixing are arguably driven by greed. However, as item B states, NMs argue that TMs are too deterministic. For example, not all working-class people commit crime even if they are in poverty. Additionally, not all capitalist societies appear to be as criminogenic as others. For example, Japan has one of the most developed capitalist economies but has a very low rate of crime. Therefore, TM theory may not be very useful in understanding the causes of crime and deviance.

> There is a good discussion here of how capitalism may be criminogenic, with some good evaluation from a neo-Marxist perspective.

Another TM view on the cause of crime is selective law making and enforcement. As the law is biased in favour of the ruling class, it will inevitably mean that the working class are more likely to be prosecuted and appear in the official crime statistics. Snider argues that the ruling class will be reluctant to pass laws that will be a threat to their profit, such as health and safety legislation. This leaves the proletariat to be exploited in the workplace and so they are more likely to be deviant and commit crime as a result. Chambliss demonstrated how colonial tax laws in East Africa protected the interests of white plantation owners. Local people had to work for low wages on the plantations as otherwise they would have been put in jail for not paying the new tax. As well as pointing out bias in law making, Marxists agree with labelling theory that the law is selectively enforced. The police will tend to ignore the crimes of the powerful and target working-class crime. This point is useful as it helps to explain patterns of crime as shown in official statistics, i.e. that the working class show higher rates of crime. However, functionalists would argue that official statistics reflect real rates of crime and that the criminal justice system is not biased and acts in the interests of everyone in society. They would also argue that rather than being made for the benefit of the ruling class, laws reflect value consensus and promote social solidarity in society. Additionally, there is evidence to suggest that the rich and powerful are subject to the law, as the scandal over MPs' expenses illustrates.

> This gives a good account of the Marxist view of bias in the law which is evaluated well from a functionalist perspective.

Another aspect of TM theory is that crime performs an ideological function for capitalism. Pearce argues that the real aim of laws seemingly passed in the interests of everyone in society (as functionalists argue) is to serve the interests of the ruling class. For example, health and safety laws give the impression that capitalism 'cares' about workers but in reality it is just keeping workers fit for work. The occasional prosecution of employers will give the impression that workers' rights are being protected. Furthermore, selective law enforcement and biased media coverage will promote the myth that crime is a working-class phenomenon. This will divert attention away from the real cause of crime which is the inequality in the capitalist system. The usefulness of this view is questioned by left realists who argue that by focusing too much on the crimes of the powerful, TMs fail to look at the fact that the main victims of working-class crime are working-class people. Additionally, as NMs argue, TMs ignore the relationship between ethnicity and crime and deviance, and the fact that individuals have free will.

> A good discussion of the Marxist view on the ideological function of crime which has some good evaluation from both neo-Marxists and left realists.

NMs such as Taylor, Walton and Young (the 'New Criminology') developed TM ideas and tried to establish what they referred to as a 'fully social theory'. While agreeing with TMs that capitalism is criminogenic, they argued that the TM view was too deterministic. They felt that individuals have free will and are able to reject capitalist values and commit crimes for political reasons. This approach incorporates TM with interactionist ideas such as labelling which can be seen as providing a useful contribution to the study of crime and deviance. This approach was adopted by neo-Marxist Hall in his study of the moral panic over 'black muggers'. He looked at how media labelling led to 'black muggers' becoming a scapegoat to divert attention away from the real problems of capitalism such as unemployment. However, the New Criminology have been criticised for only providing a framework for research and overemphasising the political nature of crime. Left realists are particularly critical of all types of Marxism (and labelling theory) for being too sympathetic to the criminal. While left realists would agree with Marxists that inequalities in society can cause crime and deviance, they would argue that crime is a real problem (particularly for those living in deprived areas) and that governments should get tough on crime as well as the causes of crime.

> A good discussion of the neo-Marxist view with some good application of a study and some very good comparative analysis with the left realist view.

Another neo-Marxist approach comes from Marxist subcultural theory which argues that working-class youth can be active and can develop styles of music, dress and language in order to resist the inequalities of capitalism. For example, Cohen argues that the skinheads in the 1970s reacted to the decline in working-class communities by wearing factory-style Dr Martens boots. These came to be seen as a part of their identity along with violent behaviour such as football violence. Similarly, Hebdige argues that youth subcultures such as punks 'resisted through rituals' by wearing bondage and safety pins, to shock the 'establishment'. However, the usefulness of these approaches has been criticised as they underestimate the extent to which these youth subcultures are influenced by popular culture and the consumerism that is promoted by capitalism. For example, some 'deviant' youth subcultures are based on corporate brands, such as followers of grime wearing Nike clothing.

> This is a good account of Marxist subcultural theory that has been applied to crime and deviance and evaluated.

Perhaps the main usefulness of the TM view is that it demonstrates how the law reflects differences in power between social class groups and how this impacts on law enforcement and the social construction of official statistics on crime. For example, the law would appear to be selectively enforced in favour of the ruling class, as white-collar and corporate crime is rarely prosecuted compared to working-class crime. This bias in the law, and the ideological nature of the portrayal of crime, can be illustrated by the different ways in which tax evasion is viewed and punished compared to benefit fraud. Perhaps the main strength of NMs is that they try to develop TM into a 'fully social' theory by incorporating interactionist approaches into studying crime and deviance. Perhaps the main weakness of the TM view is that it is too deterministic and fails to look at issues such as the fact that not all capitalist societies are as criminogenic

> This is a very good conclusion that follows the template outlined on page 51. Both Marxist views have been evaluated well with justifications given for the main strengths and weaknesses.

as others. Feminists would argue that both TM and NM ignore the patriarchal nature of the criminal justice system and how gender differences in crime can be explained by factors such as females being socially controlled by males. While NMs claim to have developed a fully social theory, it would be argued by other sociologists that it is not fully social as not all explanations are included. Right realists, for example, would argue that it ignores factors such as biological differences and the fact that crime may be just a rational choice.

This response includes a wide range of Marxist and neo-Marxist arguments on the causes of crime and deviance, which have been analysed well and applied to the question. There is a wide range of evaluation points, both specific and from different theoretical perspectives.
30/30 marks awarded

(05) Kuhn argues that science is built on paradigms. A paradigm is a framework of ideas, theories and methods that are shared by a scientific community. These paradigms allow scientists to engage in the problem-solving work of science. Kuhn believed that sociology cannot be a science as there is no shared paradigm. Sociology is made up of many different theoretical perspectives that have different explanations for social phenomena. For example, while functionalists would argue that the role of education is to instil shared values into people, Marxists such as Althusser would argue that its main role is to legitimise inequality and pass on the values of the ruling class. Additionally, feminists would focus on the way in which school reinforces patriarchal values. Even within feminism there is disagreement between radical and liberal feminists on this issue. Similarly, there is no shared paradigm in sociology in terms of the methodological approach that should be adopted. While interpretivists prefer qualitative methods as their main goal is to gain valid data, positivists favour quantitative methods to obtain reliable data. Kuhn believes that sociology can never be a science due to these disagreements over sociological theory and methods, as a shared paradigm is unobtainable.

Popper believes that science is based on the process of falsification, meaning that it has to be possible for a theory to be disproven. He regards the inductive, positivist approach as a 'fallacy'. Popper argues that a theory cannot be verified as one single observation that went against the theory would prove the theory wrong (e.g. observing a black swan would disprove the theory that all swans are white). For Popper, all knowledge is provisional, and science should be an open system which allows for this. As a result, Popper believes that although sociology can be scientific through the development of a testable hypothesis, it is generally unscientific. This is because the nature of concepts and many ideas in sociology means that they are not able to be falsified. An example of this is Marxism. Marx theorised that there would inevitably be a revolution by the proletariat but that this hasn't happened yet due to their false class consciousness. Popper argues that Marxist theory is unscientific and unfalsifiable. There is no possibility of proving or disproving his theory. Marx's prediction of a communist revolution cannot be proved wrong, nor can his view that the proletariat are being 'brainwashed' by the ruling class into not rebelling. Therefore, Popper argues that for the most part, sociology cannot be regarded as a science as most sociological theory cannot be put to the test and proved to be incorrect.

> The student has good knowledge and understanding of two reasons why sociology cannot be a science. There is appropriate application and analysis of some good examples to illustrate both points.
> **10/10 marks awarded**

(06) As stated in Item C, interactionists adopt a 'bottom-up', interpretivist approach to studying society. Additionally, interactionism is a micro, conflict theory which focuses on how individuals are labelled by powerful groups. Symbolic interactionism focuses on the meanings we attach to symbols and how this affects our behaviour. While Marxists agree that society is based on conflict, they would argue that interactionists fail to acknowledge the wider structure of society, particularly inequality caused by capitalism. However, functionalists such as Durkheim would not only criticise interactionism's emphasis on conflict in society but would also reject the interpretivist methods that interactionists tend to use. They would argue that sociologists should adopt a positivist approach to understanding contemporary society.

> This is a good introduction which follows the AAA template (see page 51).

Interactionists would reject macro theories such as functionalism and Marxism and argue that society is based on interaction and processes such as labelling. Symbolic interactionists such as Mead would argue that symbols are not fixed but have many different meanings which shape our behaviour. For example, putting your hand up could be a symbol that is interpreted in many different ways (such as putting in a bid at an auction or indicating that you want to answer a question in a classroom). Mead also argues that we are able to take on the role of 'the other' in order to understand social action. For example, we like to make a good first impression when going for an interview by dressing smartly. This is because we can take the role of the employer and know this is the image they want to see. Blumer develops this and argues that our interactions are based on meanings which we are able to negotiate. For example, a middle-class person could negotiate justice by speaking to the police officer in a certain way or by having knowledge about the legal system. According to Becker, labelling theory states that social groups create deviance by making rules that cause deviance to happen. Becker was sympathetic to the 'underdog' and felt that sociologists needed to take the side of people who may not be in powerful positions, such as working-class or black students. This illustrates how interactionism is a conflict theory and may be useful to explain issues in contemporary society such as inequality in educational achievement or in the criminal justice system.

> A good account of key interactionist arguments which have been explained with some good application of examples. The last section applies these points well to the question and has some good analysis. This paragraph could have been improved with some evaluation of these interactionist arguments.

A strength of interactionist theory is that it is 'voluntaristic'. It demonstrates how individuals have free will and are able to influence society. Goffman's dramaturgical model presents the idea of impression management — for example, a waiter will appear friendly and professional in order to get a tip from the customer. Goffman argues that we are actors who are performing roles. For example, a teacher acts differently in a classroom towards their students than they would in the staffroom with their workmates. A strength of this theory is that Goffman is right to argue that people in society act out roles. However, Marxists would argue that this ignores the power difference between 'actors' such as teachers and pupils. Structural theories reject these ideas and argue that interactionists fail to consider the wider social context in which interaction takes place. Functionalists argue that rather than being negotiated by actors, shared norms and values are given to us by institutions such as schools. As Parsons argues, the role of education is to act as a bridge between the particularistic values of the home and the universalistic values of society. By failing to acknowledge these structural factors, interactionists do not adequately explain factors that influence contemporary society.

> This paragraph outlines Goffman's version of interactionism and has some good evaluation in terms of the strength of the approach and criticisms from different theoretical perspectives.

This difference between 'micro' interactionist ideas and macro theories can be seen in the topic of education. While functionalists look at external factors such as cultural deprivation and poor values as a cause of differential achievement, interactionists place emphasis on the processes that take place within school. For example, Becker argued that teachers label working-class students as 'deviant pupils' and this led to a self-fulfilling prophecy as pupils acted out the label and would underachieve. This shows a strength of interactionism: research suggests that in contemporary society teacher labelling can have an impact on the achievement of different social groups. However, a problem of labelling theory is that it is too deterministic.

As Fuller demonstrated, students can reject negative teacher labels and develop a pro-education culture that enables them to achieve. Furthermore, functionalists would reject labelling theory by arguing that definitions come from our shared values and that labelling theory fails to explain where these labels originate from.

As Item C states, interactionists prefer to use qualitative methods such as unstructured interviews (UIs) and participant observation (PO) to understand contemporary society. This is because they allow the researcher to gain verstehen and uncover the meanings that individuals attach to their behaviour. When researching processes in schools, interactionists such as Becker use unstructured interviews to gain valid data on how teachers labelled students. Becker also used this method to uncover the 'deviant career' of drug users and how they might end up in a deviant subculture. However, as Item C states, positivists would reject methods used by interactionists as being unscientific and unreliable. They would argue that methods such as UIs and PO are too subjective and are open to researcher bias. Additionally, as they are small-scale, they are unlikely to be representative, so the findings cannot be generalised. Positivists adopt a macro approach and would argue that these methods do not show the large-scale patterns that affect contemporary society, such as the impact of religion on suicide.

When researching the topic of suicide, interactionists totally reject the positivist approach of Durkheim. Rather than using official statistics to make laws about suicide as Durkheim favoured, interactionists such as Douglas argued that sociologists should adopt a case study approach. This involved using as many qualitative methods as possible to uncover the meanings behind why a person made the decision to take their own life. For example, sociologists should study personal documents such as medical records or suicide notes, or interview the family and friends of the deceased. Interactionists would argue that this approach to research can provide insight into a very contemporary social problem. While ethnomethodologists would agree with interactionists in rejecting the positivist approach of Durkheim, they would argue that it is not possible to uncover the causes of suicide. The only thing a sociologist can research is how coroners label and come to their verdicts. They would argue that sociologists' research can show how statistics on suicide will tell us more about the way a coroner works than about actual levels of suicide. However, they would argue that the sociologist cannot begin to explain why suicide is increasing in contemporary society.

A good attempt to apply the topic of education to discuss the micro versus macro debate and outline the strengths and weaknesses of labelling theory.

This is a good discussion of the methodological approach that interactionists would use. This has been illustrated with Becker from the topics of education and crime and deviance, and evaluated with criticisms from positivists. There is some specific application to the question.

There is a good discussion here of different methodological approaches to studying the topic of suicide. Again, there is an attempt to apply this to the question.

Perhaps the main strength of interactionist theory is that it avoids the deterministic nature of structural theories such as functionalism and Marxism. For example, rather than crime being caused by structural factors such as strain or capitalism, interactionists point to the importance of labelling and societal reaction to explain why an individual is seen as deviant by society. A main strength of the interpretivist research methods used by interactionists is that they provide a rich insight into the interaction process and explain meanings for behaviour that positivist methods will not uncover. As Giddens suggests, perhaps an approach that sociologists could adopt is 'structuration', which combines both structure and action. This approach was taken up by neo-Marxists of the 'New Criminology' in their fully social analysis of crime and deviance. This combined the macro approach of Marxism with interactionist labelling theory. However, postmodernists would argue that this approach and interactionist theory are metanarratives which cannot claim to hold the truth. As contemporary society is more diverse and media-saturated, individuals can attach different meanings to symbols which cannot be easily explained by interactionist theory or research methods.

This is a good conclusion that follows the template outlined on page 51. The main strengths and weaknesses of interactionist theories and methods are suggested and explained. There is also some sophisticated analysis with the references to Giddens and the neo-Marxist approach to studying crime and deviance. It is a good strategy to refer back to the question in the last sentence of the conclusion.

Overall this shows a good range of knowledge on interactionist theory and the research methods they tend to use. Apart from the second paragraph, there are good attempts to evaluate these, and there is some good comparative analysis with other theoretical and methodological approaches. There is some good application of examples and topic areas, and each paragraph attempts to apply points specifically to the question.

20/20 marks awarded

Total score: 80/80. This response is likely to be awarded an A* grade.

Test paper 3

(01) Outline **two** criticisms of the use of situational crime prevention strategies to reduce crime.

(4 marks)

> Remember to use bullet points and give an extra point if you have time. To help gain full marks it would be a good strategy to give an example of situational crime prevention strategies to illustrate the criticism. As well as specific criticisms of policies based on the notion of 'target hardening', you could also refer to criticisms from other perspectives — for example, the left realist view that situational crime prevention strategies do not tackle the causes of crime.

(02) Outline **three** ways in which the media may cause crime.

(6 marks)

> Remember to use bullet points and give an extra point if you have time. To gain full marks you must explain how these factors cause crime. As well as ways such as moral panics, 'copycat' crime and how the media may give a distorted picture of crime, you could also refer to how advertising contributes to relative deprivation.

(03) Read **Item A** below and answer the question that follows.

Item A

Marxists argue that capitalist society is based on conflict between two social class groups. The ruling class, who own the means of production, seek to maximise profits and exploit the working class. This leads to inequalities in income and wealth. Additionally, the ruling class have the power to control institutions in the superstructure, such as the law and the criminal justice system.

Applying material from **Item A**, analyse **two** ways in which capitalism may cause social class differences in official crime statistics.

(10 marks)

> You should spend about 15 minutes on this question. Divide your time fairly equally between the two ways and write a paragraph on each. You could structure each paragraph as suggested on page 50. There is no need to write a separate introduction or conclusion. You are only required to give two ways, and these must be applied from material in the item.
>
> The first 'hook' in Item A is the reference to 'exploit the working class' and 'leads to inequalities in income and wealth'. This should lead to a discussion of how capitalism is criminogenic (Gordon). For example, you could discuss how the emphasis in capitalism on greed, profits and materialism means that crime is a rational response for all members of society. This *must* be applied to how this causes social class differences in official crime statistics — for example, how higher levels of working-class crime are a response to the poverty caused by the exploitative nature of capitalist society. This could be evaluated by reference to right and left realist arguments that the Marxist view is too sympathetic to the criminal or the view that it is too deterministic as not all poor people commit crime. The second 'hook' in Item A is the reference to the ruling class controlling 'the law and the criminal justice system'. This should lead to a discussion of how law

enforcement reflects the interests of the ruling class (Snider and Chambliss). For example, you could discuss how the law is selectively enforced, with the working class being criminalised while the crimes of the powerful are ignored. This *must* be applied to how this causes social class differences in official crime statistics — for example, how selective law enforcement and bias in the CJS can discriminate against the working class and lead them to appear disproportionally in the official crime statistics. This could be evaluated by reference to the left realist view that Marxism ignores intra-class crimes and that the CJS does act against the interests of the ruling class.

(04) Read **Item B** below and answer the question that follows.

Item B

One explanation as to why females are less likely to appear in official crime statistics is that they are treated more leniently than men by the criminal justice system. For example, women receive shorter sentences and are less likely to be sent to prison than males. Some feminists have drawn attention to the way in which females have fewer opportunities to commit crimes due to patriarchal control.

However, other feminists argue that as women become more liberated in society they are increasingly becoming engaged in risk-taking and criminal behaviour.

Applying material from **Item B** and your knowledge, evaluate sociological explanations of gender differences in offending and victimisation.

(30 marks)

You should spend about 45 minutes on this question. It may be helpful to use the template for an item-based essay question on page 51. You could start by outlining the patterns of male and female offending and refer to official crime statistics, self-report and victim studies. This should lead to a debate on the value of the 'chivalry' thesis and feminist arguments that the criminal justice system can be biased against women, particularly in sexual offences for example. You should then examine and compare explanations for gender differences in offending, such as sex role theory and different feminist explanations of control theory, liberation and marginalisation. While the main focus of the essay will be on examining explanations for females offending less than males, make sure to discuss differences in victimisation and the work of Messerschmidt on masculinity and crime.

(05) Outline and explain **two** theoretical problems with interpretivist research methods. (10 marks)

You should spend about 15 minutes on this question. Divide your time fairly equally between the two problems and write a paragraph on each. You could structure each paragraph as suggested on page 52. You should only write about two problems and there is no need to write a separate introduction or conclusion.

Make sure that you refer to theoretical problems such as reliability, representativeness, validity and objectivity rather than practical or ethical issues. You should describe each problem in some detail and use studies using methods such as participant observation (e.g. Humphries) and unstructured interviews (e.g. Dobash and Dobash) to illustrate how the problems may occur in the research process.

(06) Read **Item C** and answer the question that follows.

> ### Item C
>
> Positivists argue that sociology can and should model itself on the natural sciences and study society objectively. They believe that there is no place for values in sociology and that sociologists should discover laws about human behaviour in order to make improvements to society.
>
> However, others not only believe that it is impossible to keep values out of research but that sociologists should be committed and take the side of powerless groups.

Applying material from Item C and your knowledge, evaluate the claim that sociology can be value free.

(20 marks)

> You should spend about 30 minutes on this question. You may find it useful to use the template for an item-based essay question on page 51. You could begin by outlining the view of classical positivist sociologists who argue that a scientific sociology can be value free. This should be contrasted with Weber's view that while values can be kept out of the data collection process, they are essential in the other three stages of research. Include the debate between modern positivists and committed sociologists as well as the view of interpretivists and postmodernists. You should also include other factors that may prevent sociology from being value free, such as the influence of funding bodies and the careers of sociologists.

Student answer

(01)
- One criticism of situational crime prevention is displacement. Policies such as increasing street lighting may mean that criminals wanting to break into a car will simply move to another area that is less well lit.
- Left realists would argue that situational crime prevention does not deal with the causes of crime. Making sinks smaller in public toilets may stop the homeless bathing there but will not help them to get off the streets.

> Two appropriate points explained with examples.
> **4/4 marks awarded**

(02)
- The media may increase crime through starting moral panics. For example, Islamophobia may increase the number of religious hate crimes.
- The media may desensitise the audience by constantly showing violent images. This will mean that people come to see violence as normal which may increase criminal behaviour.
- The media may cause relative deprivation through constantly advertising the latest 'must-have' consumer goods. This may encourage the socially excluded to steal items that others have but they can't afford.

> Three appropriate points are explained with examples.
> **6/6 marks awarded**

(03) The first way that Marxists feel capitalism may cause social class differences in official crime statistics is that capitalism is criminogenic. As stated in Item A, capitalists will 'seek to maximise profits and exploit the working class'. As a result, the working class are more likely to be in poverty. As Gordon argues, crime is therefore a rational response to the inequality that will inevitably result from the capitalist mode of production. As the working class are more likely to have less wealth and be poorer compared to other groups in society, they are more likely to commit utilitarian crime and hence appear in the crime statistics. The alienating nature of work that results from being exploited might also lead to non-utilitarian crimes such as vandalism and violent behaviour amongst the working class. Marxists have been criticised for being too deterministic as not all working-class people are exploited and not all poor people commit crimes. Rather than blaming exploitation, right realists would argue that Marxists are too sympathetic to the criminal and that the working class have higher crime rates because they are poorly socialised.

The second way that Marxists feel capitalism may cause social class differences in official crime statistics is selective law making and enforcement. As stated in Item A, the ruling class have the power to control the 'criminal justice system'. Marxists argue that the law reflects ruling-class interests such as protecting private property and maintaining the profits of big business. Also, the law is selectively enforced. For example, white-collar crimes such as tax evasion and fraud are either ignored or treated less severely by the police and the courts than 'street crimes' that are associated with the working class. As a result of the criminal justice system being biased and controlled by the ruling class, the working class are more likely to appear in official crime statistics, even though they are no more likely than other groups to commit crimes. However, it could be argued that the ruling class are not always able to control the law for their own ends.

> There is good coverage of two ways that capitalism may cause social class differences in official crime statistics which follows the guidelines suggested on page 50. However, the second paragraph lacks reference to specific Marxist studies and is not as well developed in terms of evaluation.
> **9/10 marks awarded**

(04) As Item B states, females are less likely to appear in official crime statistics (OCS) than males and they receive lower sentences. Pollock argues that this can be explained by the 'chivalry thesis': that the criminal justice system (CJS) is more lenient towards women. However, as the item also mentions, feminists have different explanations for gender differences in offending and victimisation. While some argue that females commit less crime due to being socially controlled by patriarchy, other feminists point to the recent rise in female crime due to liberation.

> A good introduction that follows the template outlined on page 51.

Pollock (1950) argued that as males in the CJS have been socialised to be protective towards females, they will treat females more leniently. There is some evidence to support the chivalry thesis. Women only make up about 5% of the prison population and, as the item states, they are likely to receive less harsh sentences. For example, Campbell found that females are more likely to be cautioned than men for the same offence. Also, women are more likely to be released on bail or be given community service than males. Evidence from self-report studies also supports the view that women are treated more leniently by the CJS. Graham and Bowling found that women committed more crime than the OCS suggested in 1993. However, there is evidence that counts against the chivalry thesis. For example, self-report studies have shown that women are not treated more leniently for either serious offences (Box) or less serious offences tried in magistrates' courts (Farrington and Morris). The chivalry thesis has also been criticised for being outdated, as males are now less likely to be socialised to be protective towards females. Also, attitudes within the CJS have changed and there are more female police officers than there were in the 1950s.

> A good account of evidence that supports and counts against the chivalry thesis. There is, however, no application to the specific words in the question, i.e. 'offending' and 'victimisation'.

Further evidence against the chivalry thesis comes from feminists who feel that the CJS is biased against women, rather than treating them more leniently. Heidensohn found that courts were more severe on women in relation to sexual offences and, as Walklate suggests, it is female victims who are often 'on trial' in rape cases. However, it could be argued that the CJS is far less likely to treat women like this today. For example, the police provide counsellors to victims in rape cases. In terms of victimisation, men are almost twice as likely to be the victim of violent crimes and females are more likely to be the victim of domestic violence and sexual attacks. Feminists would again argue that the law is biased against women in crimes such as domestic violence. They would argue that the police are often reluctant to press charges for this offence, which means that the crime remains hidden and women are denied the status of being a victim of crime. Positivist victimology, on the other hand, would argue that both male and female victims contribute to their own victimisation, such as in the case of victims of domestic violence not leaving their abusive partner or males being more likely to engage in activities that will lead to becoming the victims of violent crime.

> Some good theoretical criticisms of the chivalry thesis are presented. The response has also referred to the wording of the question by discussing patterns of victimisation.

Functionalists would also reject the chivalry thesis as they would argue that the CJS acts in the interests of all citizens and is not biased in favour of females. They would argue that the reason why males offend more than females is because of differential socialisation, not chivalry. Parsons argues that, while females are more likely to conform due to being brought up to perform the expressive role, boys are socialised into being tough and taking risks, which will inevitably lead to them being more involved in criminal behaviour. Feminists would argue that differential socialisation reflects patriarchy. They criticise functionalist sex role theorists for basing their ideas on the biological assumption that females are naturally responsible for the caring, domestic role. It could also be argued that the functionalist view is dated as women are now less likely to be socialised into the housewife–mother role and to be brought up to fulfil the expressive role. As will be discussed later, this may cause females to be more likely to engage in behaviour that could lead to offending.

> There is some good comparative analysis of how the functionalist view rejects the chivalry thesis. There is some good specific evaluation of the functionalist view with criticisms from a feminist perspective.

As stated in the item, some feminists argue that as females are socially controlled by men, they have fewer opportunities to commit crime and so are less likely to offend than men. Heidensohn argues that women are controlled in all aspects of life so are less likely to offend than males. In the home, women have fewer opportunities to commit crime due to being confined to their role as a housewife. Similarly, daughters are given less freedom than sons at home. For example, they are less likely to be allowed to go out at night and so less likely to engage in criminal behaviour that may result from belonging to 'street' gangs. Due to issues such as the glass ceiling, women are less likely than males to have opportunities to commit crime in the workplace, particularly white-collar crimes such as fraud. Heidensohn also argues that generally women are controlled in society, such as not going out at night due to the 'fear of crime'. Carlen also argues that working-class women are controlled by the gender deal (emotional attachment to their partner) and the class deal (financial security). She argues that the women in her study would only commit crime when these deals break down. Most women, however, do have these 'controls' and so are less likely to offend than males. While these studies are useful in outlining how the control females experience may reduce the opportunities for them to commit crime, even Heidensohn herself accepts that they tend to portray women as passive victims of patriarchal control.

> A good account of the feminist control theory which has been evaluated and applied well to the question.

Other feminists reject feminist control theory for being outdated. Adler argues that as society is becoming less patriarchal, these controls no longer exist, and that females now have more opportunities to commit crimes. For example, Denscombe argues that girls are engaging in more risk-taking behaviour, as illustrated by the increase in 'girl gangs'. As they gain greater confidence to engage in more traditionally 'male' behaviours, this may not only lead to more criminal behaviour but also mean they are more likely to be a victim of crime. However, other feminists reject Adler's 'liberation' theory and argue that the main reason for the increase in female crime is that women are increasingly likely to experience poverty, due to issues such as the increase in lone-parent families and cuts to welfare benefits. Heidensohn argues that, rather than liberation, marginalisation (caused by poverty) has led to an increase in females offending.

> A good discussion of the debate between different feminist perspectives which again has been applied to the question.

There are explanations as to why males commit more crimes and are more likely to be the victim of most crime than females. Messerschmidt argues that the reason why men are more likely to be criminal is that they commit crime to accomplish their masculinity. Most men are socialised into hegemonic masculinity, which places emphasis on gaining wealth and power, particularly over females, and engaging in risk-taking, aggressive behaviour. As a result of trying to conform to this type of masculinity, males are more likely than females to offend and be involved in crimes such as GBH. While this demonstrates why males may be more likely to commit and be the victim of violent crimes, Messerschmidt has been criticised for not explaining why only a small number of men turn to crime to accomplish their hegemonic masculinity.

> A reasonable account of Messerschmidt but there is only a brief attempt to evaluate.

Perhaps the main strength of the chivalry thesis is that evidence suggests that historically, females have been treated more leniently by the CJS. While there is some evidence to the contrary, overall, females have been less likely to be seen as a 'typical delinquent' and therefore recorded as an offender in official crime statistics. Perhaps the main weakness of the chivalry thesis is that these theories are outdated. This criticism also applies to functionalist and feminist control theory explanations of why females offend less than males. As feminists such as Adler argue, women have become more liberated and are more likely to engage in behaviour that may cause them to offend. Alternatively, postmodernists would argue that gender roles are now more fluid and that this could impact both levels of offending and victimisation. Campaigns such as 'Me too' illustrate that females are more likely to reject being controlled by a patriarchal society in terms of being a victim of male crimes.

> This is a good conclusion which follows the template suggested on page 51. The 'something new' point on the postmodern view ensures that the conclusion refers to both offending and victimisation.
>
> This response includes a wide range of explanations of why females are less likely to offend than males. There are also some references to differences in victimisation but these, along with the explanations of males offending, could have been developed. There is some good analysis and most points have been well applied to the question. It is a good strategy to use the specific words in the question and this response repeatedly refers to the differences in offending (but less to victimisation). There is a wide range of evaluation points, both specific and from different theoretical perspectives.
>
> **28/30 marks awarded**

(05) A first theoretical problem with interpretivist methods such as participant observation (PO) and unstructured interviews (UIs) is that they lack reliability. Positivists would argue that as these methods are not standardised, they are impossible to replicate. As a result, the findings cannot be verified in a scientific way. When Dobash and Dobash used their UIs to research domestic violence, the interviews lasted for up to 12 hours, and because they lacked set questions they could go off-topic. As a result, there is no possibility that another researcher could have repeated the interview to verify that the findings were accurate. A different interviewer may not have been able to establish the same rapport that the interviews in their study were able to achieve. Therefore, the respondent may not have opened up about their experiences of domestic violence in the same way. Similarly, it is difficult to replicate PO studies such as Humphries' research on 'tea room' trade. It was difficult for Humphries to gain access to the group and it would have taken a lot of interpersonal skills to learn the procedures of the 'tea room'. It would be extremely difficult for another researcher to gain access to this group in order to replicate the study to test whether the findings were accurate.

A second theoretical problem with interpretivist methods is that they may lack validity. In terms of UIs, an issue that could reduce validity is interviewer bias. For example, in the study of Dobash and Dobash, the interviewer could have given verbal and non-verbal cues that may have influenced responses, such as asking leading questions that may have encouraged the respondent to state that their partner had been more aggressive than was the case. Also, as Oakley was a mother herself, she may have shown interviewer bias as she may have influenced the responses of the women she interviewed. Despite generally being regarded as producing valid data, the findings of overt participant observation (OPO) may lack validity due to the Hawthorne effect. As the group being studied know that they are being observed, they may change their behaviour, thus reducing the validity of the findings. In Punch's study the police officers he spent time with might not have shown him how they usually treated people during stop-and-search activities. They might have shown the 'halo effect' and wanted to appear to be fair when dealing with the public. In terms of secondary data, the personal documents that would be used by interpretivists may also lack validity. For example, a diary may appear to provide valid data and an insight into the life of the person writing it, but may include exaggerated accounts of their experiences.

This is a very detailed account of two problems. Studies are used well to illustrate the two theoretical problems raised. It is a good strategy to include at least two studies to illustrate your two points in this type of question. **10/10 marks awarded**

(06) Positivists argue that sociology can be value free through the use of objective, scientific analysis. They argue that values should be kept out of research as scientific knowledge can lead to progress in society. However, interpretivists argue that values cannot be kept out of research because the job of a sociologist is to be subjective to gain verstehen. On the other hand, others such as Gouldner and Weber argue that values should not be kept out of research as sociologists have a moral responsibility when conducting their research.

> A reasonable introduction which sets up the debate. However, it does not follow the template on page 51 as it does not refer specifically to the item.

Classical positivists such as Comte and Durkheim adopt the Enlightenment view. This argues that sociology should be value free as its job is to discover the truth about how society works in order to improve human life. In addition, sociology can be value free as we can uncover laws objectively. For example, Durkheim used secondary data to discover patterns in suicide rates which he argues allowed him to remain value free. However, his choice of topic may have been influenced by his functionalist views about society being based on social solidarity and values consensus, suggesting that his own values were not kept out of his research. Similarly, Marx saw himself as a scientist as he believed he had discovered the truth about the future of capitalist society in his theory of historical materialism. However, Marx clearly was influenced by his values as he wanted equality and to replace capitalism with communism. Again, this shows that so-called 'objective' positivist sociologists were not able to keep their own values out of the research.

> A good account of the classical positivist view on the question. There is some good evaluation and application to the question.

Weber, the founder of social action theory, argues that values can't be proven as facts by science and that sociologists need to be subjective to gain verstehen. Interpretivists agree with this approach and reject the claim that sociology can be value free. Weber believes that sociologists can't be value free when choosing a topic for research. For example, feminists believe in gender equality, which will be the main factor in influencing their choice of topic for research, such as women being oppressed in the labour market. Furthermore, he argues that researchers can't be value free in interpreting their findings and that researchers have a moral responsibility to ensure that their findings are not used in a harmful way. The only stage of research that Weber feels sociologists could be value free in is the second stage, when they carry out their research and test a hypothesis. For example, sociologists should not ask leading questions when conducting an interview. However, it could be argued that even in this stage values can't be kept out of research. For example, it could be argued that Barker did not keep her values out of her research on the Moonies as she grew too attached to the group and she may have 'gone native' as a result.

> A good discussion of Weber's stages of research which has been applied well to the question. There is some brief evaluation, but this could have been developed.

On the other hand, modern positivists argue that sociology can be value free as researchers can remain 'morally neutral' and separate their own values from the research task they are paid to undertake (e.g. by a university). However, it could be argued that modern positivists are just trying to copy science and make sociology 'respectable' when realistically values cannot be kept out of research. In addition, Gouldner argues that they conduct research to earn money from their paymasters, meaning that they will dodge moral issues which are raised. Gouldner's idea of moral responsibility suggests that values should be part of research, rather than being separated from it.

> A reasonable, if brief, account of the modern positivist view which is evaluated and applied to the question.

A further point on whether sociology can be value free is that funding bodies can influence the research process and how findings are published. For example, the Black Report was published on a bank holiday when people were less likely to read it by the Thatcher government in 1979, as its findings went against their views. This shows that values cannot be kept out of research. Furthermore, sociologists may choose areas that are 'fashionable' and may further their careers, suggesting that their research is value laden, not value free. The values of sociologists can also influence their choice of theory and research method. For example, Becker was an interactionist who was interested in taking the side of the 'underdog', so used unstructured interviews to gain verstehen on the labelling process. All this evidence disputes the modern positivist argument that sociologists can be value free in their research.

> A good summary of other factors which may influence whether sociology can be value free. While there is no evaluation, points have been applied to the question.

Committed sociologists like Gouldner argue that values cannot and should not be kept out of research as sociologists should openly take sides to support the interests of disadvantaged groups. For example, while functionalists take the viewpoint of the powerful, such as the police, Gouldner, as a Marxist, argues that we need to take the side of those 'fighting back' such as political radicals. He criticises Becker who he feels simply takes the side of the underdog and therefore does not go far enough to challenge society. However, Becker and Gouldner are both committed sociologists as they agree that researchers should take sides rather than be value free in their research. For example, when conducting research on domestic violence, sociologists should have a moral responsibility that their findings will help those being studied.

> The different views of committed sociologists have been outlined well and applied to the question.

Perhaps the main strength of the positivist argument is that research can be carried out objectively to improve society. For example, Durkheim would argue that his research could have been useful in reducing levels of suicide. However, perhaps the main weakness of classical positivists is that they were value laden rather than being value free (such as Durkheim's study of suicide being based on his functionalist views on anomie and social integration). Perhaps the main strength of Gouldner's argument that values can't and shouldn't be kept out of research is that sociologists should have a moral responsibility to ensure that their findings do not lead to harm and are used to benefit society (such as Dobash and Dobash's research on domestic violence). However, as Weber argues, it may be possible to be value free at the second stage of research, i.e. when collecting data.

This is a good conclusion that follows the template suggested on page 51. The student provides justifications of their reasons for the main strength and weakness of arguments on the question raised.

The student demonstrates a very good understanding of most of the key arguments. However, interpretivists' criticisms of the claim that sociology can be value free are only mentioned briefly. There is also no reference to the postmodern view. There is generally some very good analysis and application to the question. However, evaluation could have been developed at times.
18/20 marks awarded

Total score: 75/80. This response is likely to be awarded an A* grade.

Knowledge check answers

1 Possible answers include: they ignore female crime and corporate crime; separate subcultures do not exist.

2 Possible answers include: they illustrate how crime statistics can be socially constructed; they draw attention to the importance of labelling and its consequences; they demonstrate how agents of social control may create more deviance.

3 Possible answers include: they ignore the fact that working-class people are the main victims of working-class crime; they are too sympathetic to the working-class criminal; left realists have described the New Criminology as 'left idealism'.

4 Possible answers include: crime is a real and growing problem that is damaging communities, particularly in urban areas; individualism and the pursuit of self-interest lead to the breakdown of family structure and the community and can lead to crime; labelling and different Marxist theories are too sympathetic towards the working-class criminal.

5 Possible answers include: they are more valid than OCS as they include crimes not reported to the police; they show the 'dark figure of crime'; they have revealed how the 'fear of crime' exists in certain groups.

6 Possible answers include: canteen culture in the police; institutional racism; patterns of police labelling and stop and search; statistics on arrests, cautions, convictions and sentencing.

7 Possible answers include: some self-report studies suggest that women who commit serious offences are not treated more leniently than males; some research suggests that women are not more leniently treated in magistrates' courts; in terms of sexual offences, evidence suggests that the CJS is biased against women; the police now hold less stereotypical attitudes towards females than in the 1950s.

8 Possible answers include: they are not based on old mafia-style fixed hierarchies such as family or religion; they often involve ex-government employees; they can 'franchise' their business to other organisations.

9 Traditional criminology studies patterns and causes of law-breaking, whereas green criminology also examines the harm caused by environmental actions even if no laws are broken.

10 Possible answers include: Schwendinger's definition of human rights is too broad; there is no clear agreement on what counts as a human right.

11 Possible answers include: they are outdated as due to the diversity of new media they are less likely to be sustained in media reporting; the audience are active and are able to see through sensationalist media reporting.

12 Possible answers include: it only works on certain types of crime; zero tolerance policing has led to an increase in the prison population; it does not address the causes of crime.

13 This is when those in power achieve social control through the control of the mind (for example, through surveillance and self-surveillance).

14 Possible answers include: victim blaming; fails to examine less visible crimes; fails to take account of structural inequalities; fails to acknowledge that being a victim is socially constructed.

15 Possible answers include: both reject the economic determinism of Marx; they agree that coercion and ideology are used by the ruling class to maintain control.

16 Whereas symbolic interactionism accepts the influence of the social structure, such as the influence of social class on educational achievement or offending, phenomenologists argue that society is not 'real' but socially constructed.

17 Possible answers include: postmodernists are right to draw attention to the inadequacies of modern theories in explaining recent changes in society such as the impact of globalisation; they are right to argue that there is greater diversity and choice in society, and people are able to 'pick and mix' their own identity via the media and the consumption of cultural products.

18 Whereas the hypothetico-deductive approach of positivism argues that scientific knowledge should be based on verification, Popper argues that it should be based on the process of falsification. Rather than researchers proving their own theory, Popper argues that science should involve disproving the theories of others.

19 Whereas 'value free' means researchers should not let their personal views influence their research, 'value laden' involves sociologists making value judgements: they should be subjective and let their values guide their research.

20 Possible answers include: the cost of implementation; their own political standpoint; electoral popularity; pressure groups; global interests.

Note: **bold** page numbers indicate key term definitions.

A

Adler, liberation theory 20
Akers, labelling theory criticism 10
alienation **33**
Althusser, Louis Pierre
    law as an ideological state
        apparatus 11
    on punishment 28
    structuralist approach 34
American dream 7, 8
anomie **6**, 17, 25
    strain to anomie, Merton 7
anthropocentric view 22
Atkinson, suicide as individual act 43

B

Barrett, Marxist feminist 37
Baudrillard, 'death of the social' 39
Bauman and Lyon, liquid
    surveillance 29
Becker, labelling theory 9, 10,
    35–36, 45
Beck, on the risk society 22, 39
black feminists 38
black people, crime statistics 16–18
Blumer, concept of self 35
'bottom-up' approach
    interactionists 43
    interpretivists 41
bourgeoisie (Bs) 33, 34
Box, female crime 18
Braithwaite, disintegrative vs
    reintegrative shaming 10
Brake, Marxist subcultural theorist
    9, 12
Buckingham, media and crime 24

C

canteen culture **17**
capitalism 10–12, 28, 30–35, 37, 38
Carlen, female crime 19
Casborn, CJS is biased against
    women 18

Castells, global crime 21
Chambliss, private property laws 11
Christie, 'ideal victim' 30
class deal 19
Cloward and Ohlin, subcultural
    theory 7, 8
Cohen, A., status frustration 7
Cohen, P., working-class youth
    subculture 12
Cohen, S
    invisibility of state crimes 23
    media labelling and moral panics
        10, 25
    on social control 29
community-based policing 26
conflict subculture, Cloward and
    Ohlin 7, 8
conflict theories 32, 40
    feminism 37–38
    Marxism 33–34
consensus theories *see*
    functionalism
control theory, feminist 19
Cooley, looking-glass self 35
corporate crime 11
crime statistics 14–16
Crime Survey of England and
    Wales (CSEW) 15
criminal justice system (CJS) 16,
    18–19, 28, 29, 30
critical criminology 12
critical victimology 30
Cumberbatch, impact of media
    violence 24
cybercrime, Jewkes 24

D

'dark figure of crime' **15**
deindustrialisation **20**
dependency culture, Murray/
    Marsland 13, 17, 46
deterrence, prison as 28
deviancy amplification spiral 10, 25
difference feminists 38
displacement of crimes 27

Dobash and Dobash, study of
    domestic violence 37
domestic violence 30, 37
Douglas, subjectivity of suicide
    statistics 43
duality of structure, Giddens 39
dual systems feminists 38
Durkheim, Emile
    theories of crime 6–7
    use of comparative method 42
    views on punishment 28
dysfunctional institutions, Merton
    6–7, 32

E

ecocentric view of green
    criminology 22
ECP (environmental crime
    prevention) 26, 27
Enlightenment project 38, 39, 46
environmental crimes 22–23
ethnicity and crime 16–18
ethnomethodologists 36, 43

F

false class consciousness 33, 34
falsification, Popper 43, 44
Felson, media reporting of crime
    24
female crime 18–20
feminisation of poverty 20
feminism/feminists 37–38
    on female crime 19
    influencing social policy
        changes 46
    on science 44
    on value freedom 45
Feyerabend, nature of science 43
Firestone, radical feminist 37
'flexible accumulation', Harvey 35
focal concerns **8**
folk devils 25
Foucault, social control 28–29
the Frankfurt School 35
functionalism 31–32

explanations of ethnicity and crime 17
subcultural theory 7, 8, 9
view on moral panics 25

G

Garfinkel, use of reflexivity/ common sense 36
Garland, failure of prison in control of crime 28
gender and crime 18–21
gender deal 19
Giddens, structuration theory 36, 39
criticism by Marxists 36
Gilroy, police targeting of black youths 17
Glenny, origins of modern transnational crime 21
globalisation and crime 21–22
global risk consciousness, Beck 22
Goffman, Erving
dramaturgical approach 36
stigmatisation 9
Gouldner, value freedom 44–45
government
crime statistics 14–15
defining war crimes 23–24
social policies 45–46
state crime 23–24
Graham and Bowling, female crime 18
Gramsci, neo-Marxist humanist 34
green crime 22–23

H

Hall, moral panic over black muggers 12, 17, 18, 25
Hebdige, subcultural theory 12
hegemonic masculinity 20
hegemony **34**
Heidensohn, female crime 18, 19
Held, transnational organised crime 21
Hirschi, control theory 19, 26
historical materialism **33**
Hobbs, 'glocal' crime 21

Holdaway, police canteen culture 17
human rights 23–24
hyperreality, media creation of 39
hypodermic syringe model (HSM) 24
hypothetico-deductive model 42, 43

I

ideological state apparatuses (ISAs) 34
illegitimate opportunity structures **7**
incapacitation function of prison 28
institutional racism 17
interactionism/interactionists
'bottom-up' approach 43
explanations of ethnicity and crime 17
labelling theory 9–10
media labelling 25
social action theory 35–36
'subterranean values', Matza 8, 9
suicide statistics, Douglas on 43
interpretivism/interpretivists
feminist research 37
methodology 41
objectivity and values 44, 45
and social action theory 35
vs positivism 42–43

J

Jewkes, cybercrime 24
judicial process, racism in 17

K

Kuhn, views on science 43, 44

L

labelling theory 9–10
late-modern era 22, 39
Lea and Young
causes of MEG crime 17
exam tips mentioning 8, 15, 22, 24
victim survey, realist approach 15
left realists 10
on ethnicity and crime 17, 18
solutions to crime 26
views on moral panics 25

vs right realists on causes of crime 13, 14
legitimate opportunity structures **7**
lack of access to 8
Lemert, primary vs secondary deviance 9
liberal feminists 37, 38, 46
liberation theory 20
liquid surveillance 29
longitudinal study 40, 41
looking-glass self, Cooley 35
Lyotard, postmodernist 39, 44

M

Macpherson Report (1999) 17
Maffesoli, 'neo-tribes' 9
'malestream' theories 9, 37
marginalisation 13
Marxism 33–34
on the causes of crime and deviance 10–12
explanations of ethnicity and crime 17
subcultural theory 12
on value freedom in sociology 45
views on punishment 28
Marxist feminists 37, 46
masculinity and crime 20
mass incarceration era, Garland 28
Matza, David
neutralisation techniques 8, 23
'subterranean values' 8, 9
Mawby and Walklate, victimisation 30
McLaughlin, four types of state crime 23
'McMafias', Russian criminal networks 21
McRobbie and Thornton, moral panics 25
Mead, meaning of symbols 35
means of production **33**
the media
and moral panics 25
as possible cause of crime 24
representations of crime 24
Merton, Robert 6–7, 32

comparison with subcultural theory 8
strain to anomie: goals-and-means scheme 7
Messerschmidt, crime and masculinity 20
metanarratives ('big stories') 32, 44, 45
methodological approaches 40–41
Miers, positivist victimology 30
Miller, focal concerns 8
minority ethnic groups (MEGs) 16, 17
modern theories 38
moral panics 10, 17, 25
moral responsibility 44

N
neo-Marxism 12, 34–35, 41
explanations of ethnicity and crime 17
ideological functions of moral panics 25
neutralisation techniques, Matza 8, 23
New Criminology 12, 13
New Right 8, 46 see also right realists
Newson, media exposure and violence 24
news values **24**

O
Oakley, liberal feminist 37
objectivity in sociology 44–45
official crime statistics (OCS) 14, 15, 16, 17–18
open systems 43
opportunity structures, lack of legitimate 7, 8

P
panopticon ('all-seeing place') 29
paradigms, Kuhn 43, 44
Parsons, Talcott
pattern variables (norms) 32
sex role theory 19

societal subsystems 31
structural differentiation 32
patriarchal control, Heidensohn 19
patriarchy, feminist theories 37, 38, 46
Pearce, real purpose of laws 11
Perry Preschool project, USA 27
phenomenologists 9, 36
Phillips and Browning, MEGs 'over-policed' 16
polarisation, class **33**
police labelling 17
Pollock, chivalry thesis 18
Popper, falsification 43, 44
positivism/positivists
hypothetico-deductive model 42
methodological perspective 41
sociological research solving social problems 46
on value freedom 44
views on science 43, 44
vs interpretivism 42–43
positivist victimology 30
postmodern feminists 38
postmodernity/postmodernists 38–40
critique of functionalism 32
rejection of absolute objective truths 44, 45
subcultural theories 9
primary deviance 10
primary green crimes 22
primary methods 41
primary socialisation 31
prison, crime reduction method 28
proletariat (Ps) 33, 34
punishment 28–29

R
racism, institutional 17
radical feminists 37, 38, 46
radical victimology 30
rational choice to commit crimes 13, 14
realism/realists see also left realists; right realists

causes of crime 13–14
crime prevention 26–27
nature of science 43, 44
recidivism 28
reflexivity **36**, 39
rehabilitation opportunity, prisons 28
Reiman, crimes of the rich 11
relative deprivation 13
repressive state apparatus, Althusser 28, 34
reserve army of labour **37**
restitutive justice 28
retreatist subculture, Cloward and Ohlin 7, 8
retributive justice 28
right realists
causes of crime 13, 14
ethnicity and crime 17
on punishment 28
solutions to crime 26
risk society, Beck 22, 39, 40
Rusche and Kirchheimer, punishment 28

S
SCCP (social and community crime prevention) 26, 27
Schutz, 'typifications' 36
Schwendinger, crimes as violation of basic human rights 23
science
positivism vs interpretivism 42–43
views on nature of 43–44
SCP (situational crime prevention) 26, 27
secondary deviance 9, 10
secondary green crimes 22
secondary methods 41
secondary socialisation 31
selective law enforcement 11, 12, 17, 26
self-fulfilling prophecy 9–10, 25, 36
self-report studies 15, 17, 18
self-surveillance, prisons 29
simulacra, Baudrillard 39

situational crime prevention (SCP) 26, 27
Smart, differential socialisation 19
Snider, selective law making/ enforcement 11
social action theories 35–37
social and community crime prevention (SCCP) 26, 27
social construction
  of crime statistics 14–16
  of the news 24
  of society 36
  suicide statistics 43
  of victims 30
social control 9, 31–32
  surveillance as a form of 28–29
socialisation 13, 17, 19, 31, 37
social policy 45–46
social vs sociological problems 45
societal reaction to deviant label 9–10
South, Nigel, green crime 22
state crime 23–24
status frustration **7**
strain theory, Merton 7, 8
structural theories 31–35
structuration theory, Giddens 36, 37, 39
subcultural theory

functionalists 7, 8, 9
  Marxist 9, 12, 13
  realists' use of 14
subordinated masculinity 20
suicide statistics 42, 43
Sure Start 27
surplus value **33**
surveillance 28–29
Sykes and Matza, neutralisation techniques 23
symbolic interactionism (SI) 35

T
Taylor, impact of TNCs on global crime 21–22
theories of crime and deviance
  anomie 6–7
  labelling theory 9–10
  Marxist 10–13
  realist approaches 13–14
  subcultural theories 7–9
Tombs and White, critical victimology 30
'top-down' approach, positivism 41
typifications **9**, 36

U
underclass, Murray 8, 13, 17
utilitarian crime **7**

V
value consensus 31, 32
value freedom 44–45
verification 42, 44
verstehen, Weber 35
victimisation 30
victim surveys 14–15
violence
  and media exposure 24
  and victimisation 30

W
Walklate, victim in rape cases 18
Weber, value freedom 44
welfare state 46
white-collar crime 11
White, green crime laws, inadequacy of 22
Wilson and Kelling 26
Winlow, crime and masculinity 20
Worsley, social vs sociological problems 45

Y
Young, hippy drug users study 10

Z
zero tolerance policing 27